King Alfred
Myths and Mysteries

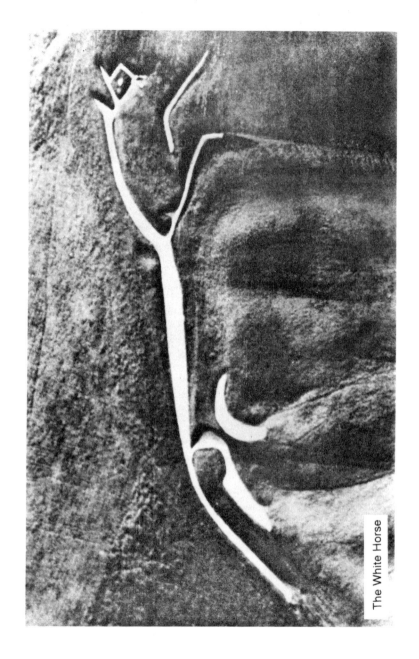

The White Horse

King Alfred Myths and Mysteries

Clive Alfred Spinage

First published in 1997
by Llanerch Publishers, Felinfach.

ISBN 1 86143 032 9

Wayland's Smithy

Contents

Maps

Preface

Until 1974 the area described in this book, now in Oxfordshire, formed part of North Berkshire for over a thousand years. A disputed territory between Oxfordshire and Berkshire for two centuries or more before this, it was then wrested from the control of the Mercians by the West Saxons. Living near the town of Wantage, the alleged birthplace of King Alfred, I received a letter from a Berkshire resident some years ago addressed to me not in Oxfordshire, but "Occupied Berkshire", which the Post Office dutifully delivered. Government recently announced that this territory will not be returned to Berkshire but will remain a part of Oxfordshire. Any study of its history can lead to confusion if the reader is not aware of this change.

As a schoolboy during the War, I was riding into Wantage on a bus with my mother. As it turned from Grove Street into the Market Place a garrulous housewife, who had been excitedly describing Wantage to a credulous American serviceman, pointed to Mill Street exclaiming: "And down there you can see where King Alfred burnt the cakes!" The American was full of wonder, and I have wondered ever since just how the woman came by that idea.

Wantage's only claim to fame is as the birthplace of King Alfred, and no-one who lives within the area can remain unaware of the Alfred connection; but the links between Alfred and the present town of Wantage may be more tenuous than are generally supposed. Recently I became interested in studying the history of a part of the area north of Wantage and I came to a conclusion which many will consider controversial, but I would not be the first to have views contrary to accepted beliefs about Alfred viewed with scepticism. In 1901 Wantage, in common with the rest of Britain, observed the milleniary of Alfred's death. But it was two years too late. The milleniary should have been observed in 1899. A leading Cambridge scholar, Stevenson, had established the true date in 1898, but his views were not accepted for many more years to come. Whether or not the reader accepts my conclusion, what is certain is that this apparently uninteresting area of the clay Vale of the White Horse is of great interest and worthy of considerably more historical and archaeological attention than it has received to date.

If I restrict myself to quoting nineteenth-century writers such as Pauli and Hughes to the exclusion of more modern authors, it is because these writers established the modern trend of what may be described as "Alfred-worship". Other writers have not been ignored, and references to many of them will be found in the bibliography.

After this manuscript had been completed Professor Alfred Smyth's blockbuster *King Alfred the Great* appeared, in which he convincingly denounced Asser's *Life of Alfred*, upon which every "Life of Alfred" to date has been based, as a forgery. In consequence, I have edited my text to conform to this and where reference is made to Asser it is in parentheses. Smyth has also shown that Alfred was by no means the saint that he was made out to be, Alfred having manipulated the media of the day to promote this saintly image of himself. This merely confirmed what I had already written in part. Alfred was great, but not perfect.

I am most grateful to the Vale and Downland Museum, Wantage, for permission to publish plates 1 and 4.

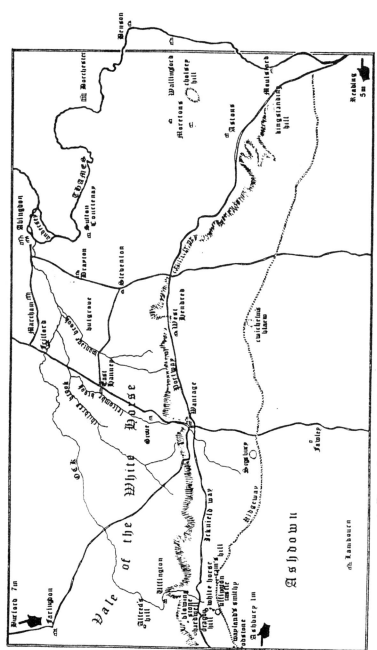

1. Downland and Vale of the White Horse. Principal places mentioned in the text.

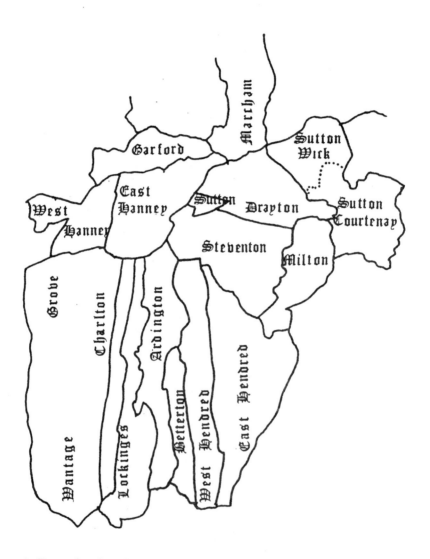

2. Downland and Vale of the White Horse parishes.

King Alfred
Myths
and
Mysteries

Chapter 1.

King Alfred's Country

The Berkshire Background

And then what a hill is the White Horse Hill!
There it stands right up above all the rest,
nine hundred feet above the sea, and the boldest,
bravest shape for a chalk hill that you ever saw.
Let us go up to the top of him, and see what is
to be found there.

Thomas Hughes. 1857.

The Top of Him

In the golden heat of one of those glorious summer days
when the larks are singing and soaring above with so much
song one fears their tiny hearts must burst, the rolling
slopes of the Berkshire Downs rise billowing like waves of
a great ocean swell frozen for all eternity into the immobile
sinuous curves of their green ramparts, echoing the evocat-
ive words of the seventeenth century poet Michael Drayton:
"...and from her steed doth showe Her lustie rising
downes."

Against this verdant backdrop with its cap of curvetting
white clouds, embedded in the soft turf enlivened by
flickering, fairy-like chalkhill blue butterflies, a curious
intrusion catches the eye of the traveller from the Vale
below. There is a strange, elongated white object, cut into
the broad shoulder of the chalk, the *albus equus* or White

Horse, the steed of Drayton's poem. Its shape and curves are such as a modern artist would have sold his soul to have created, although perhaps this shape is due more to the artistry of Time than to that of Man for:

> Before the Gods that made the Gods
> had seen their sunrise pass
> The White Horse of the White Horse Vale
> was cut out from the grass,

as Chesterton crisply put it.

It covers an acre of ground, yet you cannot see this horse, "long and wan", by looking straight up at the hillside, for it lies almost on the bald crest. Beneath it stands Dragon Hill, the bare, flat-topped, steep-sided hill shaped like a giant Christmas pudding. Legend has it that on this hill Saint George killed the dragon, although local people a century-and-a-half ago called the knight King George; probably by association with the traditional Berkshire mummer's play in which at that time King George appeared. Poisoned by the dragon's blood, it is believed grass will never again grow on the summit's sod.

Our Anglo-Saxon forebears called Dragon Hill by the Goon-like name of *Aeceles beorh.* This might have meant Eccles's Hill, or perhaps referred to a Christian shrine which had replaced a site of pagan worship, for many pagan shrines were Christianized in the second half of the fourth century and hence the allegory of St. George overcoming evil in the shape of the dragon. The dark blood of human sacrifice is much more likely to have spilled onto its summit than the blood of dragons.

Judge Thomas Hughes, the Uffington-born rector's grandson best known as the author of "Tom Brown's Schooldays", described the area as it was in 1857: ".. we

13

plodded up a gentle rise, called Sour Hill, and crossed the Iceldon or Iggleton [Ickleton] way, which I've found out since was an old Roman road; and then the ascent became quite steep, and everything was clear hill and down before us, not a fence to be seen... The road now became very bad, with ruts in the chalk like water-courses. On our left hand there was a deep narrow valley like a little bay running up into the hill, on the opposite side of which valley a large wood hung along the steepest part of the hill-side, which Joe informed me was Uffington Wood... And now the great green hill seemed to be hanging right over us, as we came to a curious round mound on our right hand.. the flat top some fifty yards across. "This is Dragon's Hill," said Joe... just below it another little deep valley, like the one on the left, only narrower and steeper at the sides, runs right up into the hill-side... "Those are the giants' seats opposite", said Joe, pointing across the valley to a set of beautiful great green slopes, like huge ridges and furrows, which went sweeping down into the valley one after another as far as I could see; "and this is the Manger, this great hole in the hill-side, because it lies right under the old Horse's nose..."

But its not all the same as it was, for even in Thomas Hughes's day Alfred's Hill had been removed to make an embankment for the Great Western Railway, completing the vandalism begun by Lord Craven about 1625. His lordship defaced it by extracting the sarsen stones to build his house in Ashdown Park as a place to escape to from the plague, "..the works are now almost quite spoiled and defaced, by digging for the Sarsden-stones as they call them, to build my Lord Craven's house in the Park." Alfred's Hill is still there in name, but as to how it acquired its name is unknown. In the 16th century it was known as Ashberry Camp, and before that the Anglo-Saxons called it *mordune* - 'the hill in the marshland'.

Yet we may still revel in the area's mysteries and delights, and anyone who stands on White Horse Hill cannot fail to be moved in heart and soul by the majesty and splendour of the vista beyond. In the words of the poet Wilfrid Howe-Nurse (1927):

> Stand on White Horse Hill,
> Watch the Vale below
> When all the world is still,
> So thou mayst know
> How brief is mortal's span,
> How weak the ruler's rod;
> How small the works of man,
> How great the works of God.

"And then what a hill is the White Horse Hill! There it stands right up above the rest, nine hundred feet above the sea, and the boldest, bravest shape for a chalk hill that you ever saw. Let us go to the top of him, and see what is to be found there... Yes, its a magnificent Roman camp, and no mistake, with gates and ditch and mounds, all as complete as it was twenty years after the strong old rogues left it. Here, right up on the highest point, from which they say you can see eleven counties, they trenched all round the table-land, some twelve or fourteen acres... The ground falls away rapidly on all sides.... here it lies, just as the Romans left it.... It is altogether a place that you won't forget, - a place to open a man's soul and make him prophesy, as he looks down on that great Vale spread out as the garden of the Lord before him, and wave on wave of the mysterious downs behind; and to the right and left the chalk hills running away into the distance, along which he can trace for miles the old Roman road, "the Ridgeway" ("the Rudge" as the country folk call it)....."

This, so aptly described by Thomas Hughes in his book "The Scouring of the White Horse", is King Alfred's country. Close by Ashdown, given by King Æthelwulf to Glastonbury Abbey in 840; where he and his brother fought the great battle against the Danes. It was long thought that *"Aelfred mec heht gewyrcan"*, "Alfred ordered me to be made", so to speak - that Alfred had the white horse cut in the chalk to commemorate the victory in 871, a theory first advanced by the Oxford antiquary Francis Wise in 1738. But recent studies date its origin to long before this, back into the Bronze Age a thousand years before Alfred fought his battle and by far the oldest chalk figure in Britain. An astonishing 3,000 years old. Although even in Hughes's day it was claimed by some to be a Celtic Bronze or Iron Age monument, and that Dragon Hill was a corruption of Pendragon, a name carried by three Celtic leaders from the time of the Roman to the Anglo-Saxon invasions. Perhaps referring to Uter Pendragon, one of those who fought the Saxons. Confusingly, excavation in 1858 turned up a Roman coin and Roman pottery, but then the Britons were not driven from the area until the middle of the sixth century, long after the arrival of the Anglo-Saxons.

The horse was not made by simply cutting away the turf, for the hill is not composed of solid chalk, and it would have disappeared long ago if this had been the method used. With their primitive instruments these late Bronze Age peoples dug out a trench and filled it with chalk. Simple enough, you might think, but it required a sophisticated understanding to construct it in such a way that it would last. Nevertheless, it has required cleaning ever since to keep it from becoming overgrown. In the 17th century Thomas Baskerville of Sunningwell in Berkshire reported that people owning land in the vicinity had an obligation to repair and clean it "else in time it may turn

16

green, like the rest of the hill, and be forgotten." The scouring of the White Horse, so vividly described by Thomas Hughes in his novel, must surely have been the oldest continuous custom in Britain before responsibility was taken over by the Office of Works this century. Wise wrote that it had been conducted from time immemorial, "solemnized by a numerous concourse of people from all the villages round about". But the meaning of the custom had long been forgotten in his day and even Wise marvelled at the custom's persistence. The last scouring accompanied by a festival was in 1857, and today's annual Uffington Show is the same as any other country show. No longer does it have any connections with its historic origins.

When cleaning lapsed after 1857 only a few years would suffice to discolour the chalk and render the outline of the Horse invisible at a distance of several miles, compared to a normal eighteen or twenty miles. When heavy rainstorms swept over the hill they would wash the chalk out and swill it down the hillside to accumulate in small heaps. All the more remarkable that it is still with us today.

But what deep emotions must have been stirred in the breasts of the first Anglo-Saxons who gazed in wonder at this representation of Woden's grey horse, Sleipnir, lying etched before them in the hillside! Admitted the horse was white, not grey, and did not have eight legs; but these would have been minor inconsistencies to a superstitious people, imbued as they were with the myths and traditions of the fearful god Woden, hunter with the souls of the dead and god of the gallows, guide and protector of military chiefs who invoked him as the god of war to awaken in the wolf warriors the berserker rage which made them invincible. To find this cryptically carved representation, only apparent if they happened by chance to approach the Downs from the direction north to east, and with the flat-topped Dragon Hill before it where the ritual propitiatory hangings which the cult of Woden demanded could be carried out, must have astonished these people from another land. Add to this the ancient belief in north Germany that the souls of the dead were ferried across the Channel to Britain like those who passed over the River Styx in Ancient Egypt, and the first Anglo-Saxon visitors to this spot must certainly have thought they had arrived in a magical land. Surely White Horse Hill and its surrounds was the most sacred place in the whole of Britain to the first Anglo-Saxons?

We know that they buried their dead on the Hill, but that there is no reference to the horse in Anglo-Saxon writings, even in the description of a boundary which passes by it, could infer that it was indeed an important pagan site, for it was against the interests of the Church to perpetuate such memories by reference to them in writing. The word 'white' may even be a corruption of *OE weoh*, 'idol' or 'shrine', and not apply to its colour at all. Not all reference to the heathen cult was expunged entirely in the conversion to Christianity, for the Wessex kings changed the pagan god into a man and claimed descent from Woden as the first great king. The adoption of this lineage may have resulted from discovering the White Horse, for the kings of Essex claimed descent from Seaxneat, a god of the continental Saxons; while the pagan Britons worshipped the god Geata, a remote ancestor of Woden.

First pointed out by the acerbic Reverend William Asplin in 1739 under the pseudonym of Philalethes Rusticus, the gangling outline has a striking resemblance to the horse on many pre-Roman British coins, crude imitations of the gold staters of Philip of Macedon which

18

depicted a horsed chariot; misleading generations of arch-aeologists into thinking that it was the Belgae who con-structed it, believing it typical of a stage of the devolution of the coin design based originally on the horsed chariot. Introduced into Gaul by Roman trade in 200 BC, these staters were imitated by the Gallic tribes, the Belgae later producing copies in Britain.

It has been suggested that the Horse might celebrate the Celtic goddess Epona, symbol of victory over life on earth known mostly from Gaul, Germany and the Danube; and in Roman times the patroness of horses, asses and mules. One thing appears certain from using the latest technology is that it was always of an abstract shape with a beaked head.

I like to think that it was meant to represent Woden's horse, the tradition of Woden stemming from Bronze Age beliefs far more ancient than those of the Teutons. We know that the cult was a hill cult, where men were sacrificed on high hills to ensure victory in battle, the top of a hill naturally being closer to the gods in the sky. Or perhaps it represents an important chief's horse which guards the Vale beneath and looks towards the chief's grave at Wayland's Smithy. Although almost two thousand years separate the construction of Wayland's Smithy from that of the White Horse, the former was no doubt still revered when the Horse was created, continuing to be an important burial site.

Or whether Bronze Age man called it Epona we shall never know, what we do know is that the hill has been called White Horse Hill and the vale the Vale of the White Horse since at least the time of Ethelred II. The ancient chronicles of Abingdon Abbey state in 978: *"juxta locum qui vulgo Mons Albi Equi nuncupatur"*, "next to a place which is commonly called White Horse Hill". And in 1100 concerning Sparsholt: *"Prope montem, ubi ad Album*

Equum scanditur, ab antiquo tempore ecclesia ista manerium, Offentum appelatum." "Called Uffington, near a hill which rises to the White Horse, of an ancient former religion."

At the beginning of the twelfth century it was listed in a book "Wonders of Britain" as the fifth wonder, but strangely referred to as "the White Horse with its foal"; and it was noted that no grass could grow on the image. The "foal" has never been mentioned since.

Much later, in Edward III's reign in 1368-9, we learn that Gerard De l'Isle held one fee in the "vale de White Horse"; franglais being even more common then than today.

Whoever created this strange "white horse", "carved rudely on the pendant sod", created it there to look out over the vast expanse of the Vale beyond, "The Garden of the Lord," as Thomas Hughes called it. Standing just above the horse's head one can see forty or fifty miles to the distant horizon on a clear day. Perhaps it was in their minds that the horse would keep watch over the Vale for them, exhilarated as they were by this heady view, just as thousands of visitors are today, aeons of time after the horse's creation.

The Earliest Men and Monuments

After the end of the Ice Age, some 12,000 years ago, when Stone Age Man moving northwards from the Continent began to colonise this area, we would have seen in the Vale an extensive woodland of oak and ash, intersected by broad seasonally inundated reedy marshes fringing the lowland

20

streams such as Cow Common Brook, Childrey Brook and the River Ock. The first colonisers probably lived on the higher, drier ground, halfway up the Downs, descending to hunt in spring to autumn. Their worked flints are widely scattered in the Vale, which was home to the dreaded wolf, the great wild ox - the aurochs, and the red deer; remains of both of which latter beasts have been found used by Middle Neolithic man about 3,500 BC near Abingdon.

Near to Wantage, two hundred and fifty years ago, a human skeleton was found in one of the barrows on the Downs, the antlers of a deer buried with it perhaps signifying a great hunter or some connection with the ancient superstition of Herne the Hunter of the Berkshire forests. The bow and arrow was the principal weapon for hunting, and flint arrowheads were still in use for many centuries after the first introduction of bronze; but even in the Iron Age there are few remains of game animals to be found compared with those of sheep and cattle. Red deer, roe deer and hare, form less than 3% of remains found.

Until metal came into general use these men could make but little headway against the forest, although the earliest Neolithic occupants on the Downs already possessed small cattle, horses, pigs, goats and dogs. By at least the Middle Neolithic these animals were being farmed in the Vale at and near Abingdon.

By 1000 BC White Horse Hill had been cleared of forest, but the earliest monuments in the area date back over 5,000 years, Lambourn Barrow being almost 5,500 years old, more than a thousand years before the end of the Neolithic or Late Stone Age. Celtic migrants from Europe then arrived heralding a new age known as the Bronze Age from their already accomplished use of this metal. Some five hundred years later they had probably already cleared vast areas of woodland to make way for shifting cultivation

21

and grazing, creating a mosaic of vegetation types with open country and light woodland now covering the higher ground.

By about 2,500 BC land use by these early farmers is believed to have involved a gradient from the crest of the Downs descending to a river or stream in the Vale with the living sites on the lower slopes, above the wetter levels which would have been infested with malaria-carrying mosquitoes in the summer months. Although at this time the Thames Valley floodplain was drier and better drained than it was to be later when rainfall increased, in autumn and winter the lowest level would often have been flooded and the cattle and sheep would be moved to high ground. As the marshy flats dried out the stock would move back down again and graze them in the spring to autumn.

Forest clearance appears extensive in the Neolithic and Bronze Ages, and in the late Bronze Age and early Iron Age farming settlements became more numerous, agriculture spreading from the light upland soils to the clays and wetter floodplain soils, coinciding with a rise in the water table which at the same time pushed people back from the riverside plains. But the people particularly favoured the high ground of the rolling chalk downs with its absence of malaria and pestiferous swamps. In the Vale their cattle and sheep would die of diseases such as anthrax and lungworm infection, yet remains of their former presence in the lowlands is numerous nonetheless because the pastures there were much richer.

The water meadows in this part of the country have traditionally provided early grazing for sheep and cattle in the spring. Not until the eighteenth and nineteenth centuries did much drainage take place so that the previous marshlands, the meads adjacent to the brooks, disappeared. But flooding of these low-lying areas still takes place in very wet years.

These industrious proto-peasants were the people who constructed the oblong burial mounds of the Downs. Wayland's Smithy was one such megalithic burial chamber, exposed since man's memory of it began, but in the early 19th century a large quantity of the stone was also taken away to build a barn. Its cruciform rocks were probably originally covered with earth, exposed when it was plundered, the building of it perhaps influenced by the pyramids of Egypt which were being constructed contemporaneously. In Britain they did the best that they could with the materials and labour available to them, so that the pyramids of Wessex were the great barrows on the Downs, the densest concentration in Europe.

Here in Wessex, in what has been aptly termed the cradle of British prehistory, the grizzled rocks with their hoary mysteries of the legendary Wayland Smith's Cave are the remains of a Middle Neolithic barrow dating from about 2,800 BC, pre-dating the first Bronze Age arrivals and far, far older than Stonehenge. At least 14 persons, mostly young adults together with one child of about 9 years of age, were first buried in an earthen barrow at the site of the latter, together with three flint arrowheads. Within a century a stone chamber reached by a passageway had been erected and at least 8 persons with a child laid to rest in the chamber. Erecting the facade of great sarsen stones is calculated to have required 35 to 50 able-bodied men.

It is believed that the bodies were first left to partially mummify on a wooden platform supported between two vast tree-trunk pillars which would have been visible for miles over the countryside. For such a burial these must have been important people, probably a chief together with his family and servants killed at his funeral and buried with

23

Ch1

him. For all we know buried with great treasures like some Egyptian pharoah, for there is evidence to suggest that the tombs had already been plundered in the Romano-British period. In the seventeenth century the arrangement of the stones was described as so disorderly that one would imagine they had been tumbled out of a cart; and the following century it was plundered for a different reason, some of the stones being broken up to mend the roadways.

The huge sarsen stone circles of Avebury and Stonehenge came a thousand years later, with peoples who worshipped the sun and had affinities with others of like mind from western Asia. The ancestors of those who built the barrows originated from the Mediterranean region, and like their Nile brethren they worshipped the dead and believed in reincarnation. Just as they watched each spring succeed each winter and the skeletons of dead trees like the mighty oak burst into life again. Their trade links extended, we know, to Ancient Egypt; for blue faience beads from there have been found among their grave goods.

That the name of Wayland's Smithy is of great antiquity we know from the first reference, *Welandes smiththan,* in a charter of 955 describing the boundaries of the Parish of Compton. The legend of Wayland was popularised by Sir Walter Scott in his romance "Kenilworth" in 1821, but recorded a century before by Francis Wise: "All the account, which the country people are able to give of it, is 'At this place lived formerly an invisible Smith; and if a traveller's Horse had lost a Shoe upon the road, he had no more to do, than to bring the Horse to this place, with a piece of money, and leaving both there for some little time, he might come again and find the money gone, but the Horse new shod.'"

Thus here, on the Berkshire Downs overlooking the Vale of the White Horse, was a part of the timeless mythology of Scandinavia enshrined, keeping alive an ancient Teutonic mythic tradition. We undoubtedly owe its remembrance to the Anglo-Saxons who loved to dwell on these ancient tales as children thrill today to the stories of Tolkien. In the Anglo-Saxon romance of Beowulf the hero's favourite breast-plate was made by Weland, "it is the legacy of Hraedla, the work of Weland." King Alfred, translating the Roman Boethius's "Consolation of Philosophy" from the Latin, not, as some scholars thought, mistaking Fabricius for "fabricator" or "smith", hinted at his knowledge of Wayland's Smithy by calling Fabricius Weland, in order to give the translation a local flavour, writing: "Where are now the bones of the celebrated and wise goldsmith Weland?...Where are now the bones of Weland? or who knows where they were."

Weland, the Teutonic version of the Greeks' Hephaestus or the Romans' Vulcan, was an armourer, in some traditions a "lord" of the elves who had obtained from hobbit-like creatures in the interior of the mountains, the dwergr or dwarfs, great skill in the working of metals by fire. Falling into the power of the wicked Swedish king Nidud, he was employed in making wonderful weapons and jewels, but that he might never escape the king had him hamstrung and the muscles of his feet cut, laming him for life. Eventually Weland found an opportunity of paying back the king by slaying the king's two sons and raping his daughter, before flying away on wings which he had constructed. But not before he had made the skulls of the king's sons into magnificent, gold-decorated, drinking cups; which the king unwittingly used at his table.

Berkshire people did not know of this story, their legend of Wayland came from another Scandinavian folktale, for it is the mythical story of Theodoric, the sixth century German king of the Ostrogoths who somehow became mixed up in Scandinavian folklore as a smith who, in penance for blaspheming on the death of his wife, was imprisoned in a cave and shod the horses of passing travellers in the same covert manner.

But Berkshire people also had another legend concerning Wayland, that he was plagued with a disobedient apprentice, by name Flibbertigibbet, who, one day, tired of being chastized by his master, ran away. When he was about a mile distant, the angry Wayland cast a huge stone at him which rolled down the hillside and struck poor Flibbertigibbet on the heel with such force that he left the print of his foot on the stone. Flibbertigibbet sat down and cried at this hurt, and to this day the point is known as Snivelling Corner (perhaps from Old English *snad* - a detached piece of woodland), the stone lying in the corner of a field of Oldstone (Odstone) Farm. A settlement since at least Roman times, the mediaeval village was abandoned by the beginning of the sixteenth century.

How much of this story was due to the imagination of Sir Walter Scott and how much might be local legend is questionable. Flibbertigibbet was a sixteenth century name for a gossipy woman, although Shakespeare in King Lear applied it to a fiend. In nineteenth century Berkshire dialect, flibberty-gibberty meant flighty or unreliable; but in eighteenth century southern Norway folklore Madame Flappetylappet, so called on account of her long tail, was a kind of witch who led the wild host of the wicked dead who were condemned to ride about until the end of the world. Christmas was their favourite time of the year for showing themselves.

Huge sarsen stones or "grey wethers", lumps of hardened sandstone which once overlay the chalk, lie scattered on the Downs and many have strange legends attached to them. There are those at Ashbury said to be sheep petrified by Merlin, King Arthur's magician. Others know them as Druid stones, thought to have been connected with pagan Iron Age worshippers. Local people believed that they grew out of the ground, which in a sense they do, gradually coming to the surface due to weathering away of the topsoil and contraction of the ground in winter frosts.

If you began a journey at Thomas Hughes's village of Uffington as one would have done in his day (not named after the Mercian king Offa but after one Uffa when the estate of *Aescenburh* or Ashbury was divided after 953), not so sleepy nowadays but still with his childhood chalk-stone school and quaint ancient thatched reminders of a more leisurely age, following the narrow tree-lined road towards Ashbury, *Aescesbyrig* or "Ash tree camp" as it was known in the ninth century the name the Anglo-Saxons gave to Uffington Castle, at the foot of Blowingstone Hill you would happen upon the Blowing Stone, the strangest of the sarsen stones and a relic associated in popular belief with Saxon times. If you are possessed of lungs enough to blow sufficiently hard into the hole in the top of this hundredweight stone, it will emit a mournful boom audible up to a mile away, and possibly twice that on a still day.

The only true blowing-stone in England, legend has it that it once stood up on the Downs and was used as a war horn to summon Anglo-Saxon armies to battle. King Alfred's Bugle horn some called it, but our first known reference is on John Rocque's map of Berkshire of 1761, where the name of 'Blowingstones' appears. Yet Francis Wise, who delved deeply into local tradition, did not mention it 23 years before, so the Alfred tradition is unlikely to have been associated with it then. The stone is believed to have been brought below and placed in its present position about 1760 by a local landowner. Whoever moved it apparently realised its significance, after all, people do not just go around trying to blow into stones to see if they make a noise; but this significance is now lost to us. More likely Druidical priests sounded a sacrificial death siren with it in some bloody rite, rather than Alfred summoning his troops to the Downs with a bugle call to arms.

The Castle Builders

About 2,600 years ago the Bronze Age peoples, who had already undergone settlement contraction due to climatic deterioration beginning about 1,000 BC, with wetter and colder conditions more similar to today's, were replaced by the Iron Age invaders from Europe. Three waves of these new immigrants took place, the third comprising the mixed Celto-Germanic Belgae about 75 BC. Those who inhabited Berkshire comprised a tribe known as the Atrebates, whose chief city was Calleva (Silchester in Hampshire). To the north, in Oxfordshire, were the Dobunni. From the relative occurrence of their respective coins, the Vale of the White Horse appears to have lain between the two tribal areas, but that does not mean to say that it was a "no man's land". These Belgae were not the primitive savages that Caesar made them out to be when he invaded Britain in 55 and 54 BC, but an industrious people with a culture of their own, albeit not as advanced as that of the Romans. Caesar's visit was little more than a reconnaissance, and it was to be a hundred years later before the Romans definitively invaded Britain.

With the Iron Age people came a return to permanent upland habitation, and instead of a pastoral nomadic people a settled agricultural population with cultivation in terraces came into being. But whereas it was formerly thought that these people only favoured the higher ground of the Downs where they constructed their hill forts, there is ample evidence of widespread living in the lowlands of the Vale as well. The landscape was now more systematically divided, delineated by trackways and rectangular enclosures.

Despite the industry which these people showed, the Downs were a bloody place in the Iron Age before the Romans came, for, if we can believe it, Iron Age worshippers were still eating their young virgins two thousand years ago, killing them in bloody ritual massacres in dark, satanic groves. These groves were often a clump of trees on a high point of the Downs, such as we see still standing on the hilltops today. But these people were fighters and built not barrows for their dead, but great earthen hill forts to defend the living. Massive hill-top fortresses which were probably to protect tribal areas, continuing to develop them up to the time of the Roman invasion.

Uffington Castle was an example of such a hill fort built about 500 BC. A major fortified site, it is situated on the highest part of the chalk scarp on White Horse Hill beside the prehistoric Ridge Way or *hrycwaeg*, commanding extensive views northwards over the Vale. A plain of more than eight acres in extent at the highest point in the area is surrounded by earthworks comprising a bank eight or ten feet high in places, and a single broad deep ditch, twenty-five feet to its bottom from the top of the inner bank. Outside of this is another large bank of earth, seemingly originally with a timber rampart replaced in 300 BC with one of sarsen stones; and from the foot of which the Downs fall away on every side. Three entrances are cut through the double banks: one each on the west, south-east and north-east sides. Its large size is attributable to the fact that, in time of attack, the people would drive within the fortification all of the stock upon which their survival depended: cows, sheep and pigs. Abandoned about two thousand years ago, it was later used in the Roman period at first for an unknown purpose and then as a cemetery.

In the even bigger Segsbury Castle south of Wantage, last century an eighteen-inch conical stone was discovered standing above a small chamber walled with flints, with a floor of a single slab of stone. In the cavity thus formed were human bones, some flint instruments and a fragment of pottery. Baal, the god of the Phoenicians, was worshipped under the form of a conical stone.

About a mile west-north-west of Uffington Castle lay Hardwell camp, also with earthworks; and a mile to the south-west was a third, smaller, circular camp, known as King Alfred's camp. Not far to the east stands another smaller one known as Ram's Hill, a corruption of the Anglo-Saxons' *hremnes byrig* or Raven's camp, of similar construction in a scarp-top position. Here Romano-British burials have been found in a square-ditched enclosure abutting it. Another fortified site near Uffington, of which no above-ground structure remains today, was known in Anglo-Saxon times by the quaint name of paddebyrig, or "toad camp".

The Belgae built hill forts concentrated on their tribal frontiers for defence rather than as the tribal capitals their Iron Age predecessors had in their early stages. But whom were the forts such as Uffington Castle to defend against? Tribes in the Vale or tribes coming from the south? Or were they simply to police the Ridgeway?

The Ridgeway, or Rudgeway as the locals called it in Thomas Hughes's day, may have originated in the Bronze Age or in Neolithic times, but seems to have changed course considerably since the 18th century. Beginning as a broad zone, already in prehistoric times it gradually became restricted by farming. There is no evidence of trade along it.

Roman and Anglo-Saxon

In AD 43 the Romans definitively invaded Britain, using the Thames to penetrate westwards as the Saxons were to do after them. They allegedly built their straight roads for military campaigns during their conquest after AD 43, but it now seems that in many instances they simply followed already-existent Bronze Age roads. In addition to better-known places such as Dorchester, sites such as Oxford and Abingdon became important Roman centres, Abingdon developing on an Iron Age fortification. Although the bridge over the River Ock on the Roman road from Wantage to Oxford has long been known as the site of a Roman ford with a temple nearby, in recent years a large amphitheatre was discovered there, comparable to that at Pompeii and showing that the whole of this area in the Vale must have been of considerable importance, attracting large numbers of people.

Roman villas dating from about AD 200, found scattered on the Downs and in the Vale, were probably inhabited by wealthy British gentry rather than by Romans. The Britons or Celts were not driven from the Vale until the middle of the 6th century by the Anglo-Saxons, two centuries after the Romans had left. Due to the low population density, few Anglo-Saxon remains are to be found and we first read of Ashdown or *Aescesdun*, "the hill

31

of the ash", in 648 when Cuthred, who had been driven from the throne for rejecting Christianity and repudiating his wife, was reinstated and granted 3,000 hides near *Aescesdun* by his kinsman King Cenwealh of the Gewisse, the tribe of Anglo-Saxons which occupied the area of the Upper Thames Valley.

The area Cenwealh granted is considered suspiciously large, exceeding the 10th century hidage of the whole of Berkshire. If the figure was not inflated in the telling then it would have covered the whole of the Berkshire Downs and the Vale, as well as part of north Wiltshire or west Oxfordshire. In the year 840 Æthelwulf, King of Wessex, gave 10 cassatos (hides), i.e. probably 1200 acres, of land at 'a place called' *Ayshedoune* to his minister Duda, but about 900 the name *Aescesdun* seemed to apply to the whole line of the Berkshire Downs.

Ashdown may well have been the territory of Cwichelm, King of the West Saxons, who died in the year 636 immediately after his conversion to Christianity. The hill known as *Cwichelmes hlaew* or Ashdown, or today variously as Cuckhamsley Hill or Scutchamer's Knob, lying just to the west of the new landmark of the Harwell Atomic Energy Establishment, was a well known landmark in Anglo-Saxon times with its own special aura and folklore. *Hlaew* meant a tumulus built or re-used for Anglo-Saxon burial, this one dating from at least Iron Age times. By 990 it had become a meeting place of the Shire which the Danes went out of their way to discredit in 1006. It had been put about that if the Danes reached there they would never get back to the sea again, so having pillaged Reading and Wallingford, after spending a night at Cholsey, out of bravado a raiding party camped the following night at the *hlaew* - and reached the sea again.

Cenwealh, brother of Cwichelm, succeeded to the

32

throne and went on to build up Wessex, reigning for more than thirty years until he died suddenly in 672. Without children or lineal descendants he had committed the administration of his kingdom to his wife Sexburh, who took the head of the army. Within a year she had been either killed or deposed and two lesser kings or chiefs, Aescwine and Centwine, the latter apparently the rightful heir to Cenwealh, governed or rather attempted to govern; for there followed ten years of anarchy.

Although the Gewisse of Hampshire and Wiltshire were a force to be reckoned with after the 680s, the Mercian kings never fully subdued them, but the Vale was one of the areas which the Mercian kings managed to hold on to for most of the time. The West Saxon kings Caedwalla (686-8) and Ine (688-726) beat the Mercians back from south Berkshire but apparently did not succeed in pushing them, at least not permanently, out of the Vale. The entire area between the Cotswolds and the Berkshire and Wiltshire Downs was probably highly unstable, under heavy Mercian influence even when Wessex controlled it. Offa, the most powerful of the Mercian kings, appears to have recovered the Vale about 779 when he attacked Cynewulf at Benson. An Abingdon chronicler, writing several centuries later, alleged that Offa then gained the territory between the Thames and the Berkshire Downs Ridgeway, westwards to the later Wiltshire boundary.

King Æthelwulf of Wessex made grants of land in the Vale in 840 and 856, and West Saxon control of the Vale was consolidated when King Burgred of Mercia (852-74) married King Æthelwulf's daughter Æthelswith. Bishops of Mercian sees never again had authority over Berkshire, which was absorbed into the Winchester diocese and transferred about 909 to a new West Saxon see eventually fixed at Ramsbury in Wiltshire. The Thames emerged by

33

negotiation, not by conquest, as the definitive frontier between the Mercian and West Saxon kingdoms.

The Land of the Vale

The parishes on the northern slopes of the Downs run down in narrow parallel strips to the Vale below. This arrangement, seen in the shapes of Wantage and Charlton, Lockinge, Ardington, and West Hendred; was once attributed to the Bronze Age system of a family or group exploiting the different levels through the seasons. Historians then thought, from the evidence of aerial photographs, that these early field systems were not linear but, in use well into the Roman period, rectangular. Now, it seems, the Romans may have created the rectangular field systems. These, it was thought, were cut across in the early Anglo-Saxon period about the seventh century by estate boundaries which divided them into further rectangular-shaped holdings on which ecclesiastical parishes were based. This was followed by progressive linear subdivision as large estates were split up and given away between the 950s to 980s, the linear nature of these holdings relating to frontage to the streams flowing down the hillside. In fact, this pattern seems to follow the original Romano-British divisions, the Anglo-Saxons simply adopting them with little further division. When we get to the lowlands we find the tendency of parishes to be elongated in an east-west direction along the rivers.

Soil washing into the Thames increased rapidly after the 9th century, which means that its tributaries were perhaps much more open two centuries earlier. This increase in run-off meant that there had been a great increase in tillage, particularly on the high ground. When the Anglo-Saxons arrived most of the woodland had long been cleared, the country already open in Roman times. No woodlands are recorded for this part of the Vale in the Domesday Survey of 1086, but this has been shown to be deficient for other parts of the Oxford region, where eleventh and twelfth century Abingdon charters show that areas were well-wooded which are not recorded as such in Domesday. Nevertheless, like much of Berkshire, the landscape was probably bleak, created by centuries of uncontrolled grazing, particularly by pigs, with Wantage Brook meandering through a broad marsh. Yet by the time of the Survey, the Vale had become one of the most populous and prosperous parts of Berkshire; with settlements on the islands - Hanney, Goosey, Charney - and at the fords - Lyford, Garford, Frilford, and Appleford. The islands had perhaps become attractive because of their defensibility, originally no more than temporary refuges from the Danes; while the fords would have been guarded by military camps, leading to permanent settlements.

On a clear day I look up from my house in the Vale at ten miles of rolling green Berkshire Downs, reaching before me across the horizon from Chilton, the ceorls' town, in the east, beyond the royal ham of Wantage in the west to the heights of Lambourn, another Anglo-Saxon royal ham. Turning my back on this undulating rampart, to the north of me stretch the hills of the grim-sounding Corallian moors, with Oxford and her dreaming spires hidden beyond Boar's Hill, wooded even today. Was somewhere in this great flat Vale which lies between, Alfred's birthplace? If it were, I do not believe it to have been where Wantage stands today.

Alfred, we are told, was born at Wantage, just under the lea of the Downs which were to see so many bloodthirsty battles. *"In villa regia quae dicitur Wanating in illa paga, quae nominatur Berrocscire; quae paga taliter vocatur a berroc silva, ubi buxus abundantissime nascitur."* wrote "Asser", Alfred's fictional biographer. "He was born in the royal villa called Wantage in that country which is called Berkshire, which country is so named from the wood of Berroc, where grows the box-tree in great plenty." But he was wrong to translate berroc as box, the word really meaning hilly, or "the hilly shire". Not an Anglo-Saxon but a Celtic word, which "Asser", if he had been a Welshman as was claimed, ought to have known. Box is a rare species in Berkshire although there once was a wood of it near Reading, grubbed up in the mid-eighteenth century.

The most recent authority disputes Wantage as Alfred's birthplace (1), but if Alfred was not born there, this is still Alfred's country, if not the boyhood home of England's greatest king. Not far from Wantage lies Grove, or King's Grove to give it its old name. Alfred was said to be an "unrivalled hunter", an attribute ascribed to almost all kings, but if indeed he hunted, then perhaps it was here in this now unprepossessing dormitory of Wantage, then a flat, wooded land, with the Letcombe Brook winding through it, that he may have sought his quarry, for grove or *grafe* means a wooded area.

"What were the first impressions which must have influenced the spirit of this child? Surely they were the invigorating pictures of surrounding nature, the verdant woods and fields, the blue sky with its clouds driven over the island by the fresh breezes..." romanticized the German historian Pauli. Alfred, he imagined, "throve visibly in the free air and amid the din of war, more beautiful than either of his brothers, more loveable in speech and demeanour. His gentle disposition lent a singular charm to his innate desire of doing honour to his noble descent by the culture of a noble spirit." The culture of youth, we are told, "consisted only in the strengthening of the body by warlike exercise and the chase, and in all Teutonic nations the mind was early quickened by the songs and poems of the fatherland."

Note

1. Smyth, A. P. 1995. King Alfred the Great. I argue for Wantage as the birthplace in Chapter 6.

Chapter 2

The Alfred Inheritance

Background to the Anglo-Saxons

Public as well as private buildings were overturned;
everywhere the priests were cut down before the altars...nor
was there any to bury those who had been thus cruelly
slaughtered. And thus some of the miserable survivors,
being captured in the mountains, were butchered in heaps;
others, spent with hunger, came foward and submitted to
the enemy, to undergo perpetual servitude for the sake of
obtaining food, if they were not killed on the spot...

Bede. AD 731.

Bloodthirsty Pirates

Despite the Venerable Bede's lurid account of the first
attacks of the Anglo-Saxons on the Britons, Alfred liked to
imagine he had descended from a bold, conquering army
which had invaded Hampshire fighting its way to greatness.
As the Anglo-Saxon Chronicle described it, "proud assail-
ants, warriors eager for glory, overcame the Britons and
won a country."

"What the books tell us and our ancient sages" had it
that in the year 495 two bloodthirsty German pirates landed
on the south coast of Britain with five ships. These were
Cerdic and his son Cynric. Of course the legends did not
call them bloodthirsty, nor pirates - but warriors. Followed
by hordes of kindred spirits over the next ten years, these
fearless people conquered their way step by bloody step,

38

fighting many desperate battles, and, distinguishing themselves by their fierceness and recklessness, bit by bit they seized the country from the hapless Britons. They fought not only Britons who opposed them, but others of their own kind who came from the west. Britons, Celts, and the Jutes who had landed in Kent and on the Isle of Wight; all were driven before them in their relentless pursuit.of plunder. These savage adventurers were, legend has it, the founders of Wessex and the ancestors of Alfred.

Cerdic lived for forty years in England, the last sixteen as king of the West Saxons, ruling Hampshire, Dorset and a part of Somerset. Central Hampshire, Wiltshire south of Ashdown and probably the middle Thames Valley, became the West Saxon kingdom under him about 520. Once he had attained power, as is usual amongst conquerors, he then claimed descent from a royal line, tracing his ancestry back to the mythical Teutonic pagan god Woden himself.

After the death of Cynric, who had succeeded his father and ruled for twenty-six years, the place of king was taken by Cynric's son Ceawlin. Ceawlin raised Wessex to the highest position amongst the neighbouring kingdoms, adding the Upper Thames Valley, including Wiltshire north of Ashdown, and drove the Britons into Wales. But for the next three centuries the land was thrown into a turmoil which we may liken to that of Angola or Mozambique in modern times, as the descendants of Cerdic strove each against the other for power. Cynric, Ceawlin, Ceolric and Ceolwulf followed, all fierce and bloody pagan warriors, keeping out of Wessex the missionaries of the day who sought to convert them to Christianity.

Then, not long after the year 628, pagan Hwiccan or Mercian royalty annexed west Oxfordshire, and in the next half century it was colonised by the now Christian Hwicce, the tribe which inhabited present-day Worcestershire,

Gloucestershire and Warwickshire.

After the death of Ceolwulf in 611 rule of the kingdom was split up into many parts, one of which was ruled by Cynegils, who, in 635, thirty-eight years after Augustine had landed on the Kentish coast, was baptized by St. Birinus at Dorchester. It was not until Egbert came to England in 802 and was made king of Wessex, following the death of Beorhtric, that the crown at last descended on the heir who was able to ensure its succession in his own family.

In the next twenty years Egbert extended his power to embrace not only Hampshire, Dorset, Somerset and the Isle of Wight, but the whole of the land south of the Thames to the sea, adding Berkshire, Wiltshire, the southern half of Oxfordshire, the greater part of Gloucestershire and the whole of Devon. Instead of many chiefs or sub-kings, there was now one supreme ruler; and the nobles, freemen and serfs in all of the hitherto separate districts, began to be welded into one cohesive community. But Egbert was not to enjoy his success for long, for other rapacious invaders were casting covetous eyes on England's fair fields.

In the year 835 the Danes devastated the Isle of Sheppey, an attack which was to herald the beginning of a long and bitter struggle lasting for 180 years until the Norse king Canute conquered England in 1016. Although the Germanic invaders were nothing more than bloodthirsty barbarians, "skilled in the Germanic mode of warfare" as Pauli puts it, mercilessly overcoming the placid Britons who had had four hundred years of stability under Roman rule, the Danes were to become labelled the barbarians; and the previous invaders, the Anglo-Saxons, were to become cast in the role of the saviours of mankind.

The Infiltrators

The reality behind the establishment of the Anglo-Saxons in Britain was different to the tale of the conquering warriors of Cerdic and Cynric. Up to the sixth century, the annals in the ninth century Anglo-Saxon Chronicle which has come down to us, are now regarded as largely unreliable, possibly containing no useful information at all. The main purpose of the Chronicle at its outset, which bears the hallmark of being instigated by Alfred, was to glorify the ninth-century kings of Wessex and their ancestors, the kin of Cerdic, particularly Alfred himself. Stories of different groups were linked together to create a single history of Alfred's supposed ancestors expanding from a Hampshire base. The main scene of the action is now recognised as having been the Upper Thames in Oxfordshire, not Hampshire and southern Britain.

During the Roman occupation of Britain, their own troops being thin on the ground, the Romans employed a number of Saxon or German officers; imported barbarian mercenaries whom they could trust to command outposts or detachments throughout the country. When the Roman ruler Constantinus, who chose to spend the greater part of his life in Britain, died at York and his son Constantine was proclaimed emperor, it was a German prince who supported the nomination. After the Roman ruler Constantine III (no relation to the former) departed for Gaul in 407 never to return to Britain, taking his troops with him to combat the threat of invasion by hordes of Germanic tribes who had crossed the frozen Rhine, the peoples of the North Sea Coast of Holland and West Germany became bent on seizing this now undefended rich and prosperous land for permanent settlement. Instead of as heretofore indulging in mere piratical incursions.

The first of these invaders were few in number. Some settled peacefully alongside the Britons, but others fought for their footholds. As immigrants who arrived with women and children and all of their possessions, there was no turning back. Roman Britain had suffered attack from sea pirates; Picts and Scots; as well as the North Sea coastal peoples collectively known as Saxons; since the later third century AD. But now the would-be immigrants were desperate. Piracy was no longer mere adventure but a necessity. War had destroyed their once-prosperous trade with the western Roman provinces, and a rise in sea level continuing up to the fifth century inundated their low-lying villages on formerly fertile land along the North Sea coast. To them there was no alternative but emigration, and they had learnt of the richness of Britain from their brethren who served there under the Romans, as well as from their pillaging excursions. So more and more immigrants poured into the area around the Wash until quite late into the fifth century in a bid to occupy what they now saw as the promised land.

Shortly after the first arrivals, some sailed up the Thames and settled at Dorchester, to be reinforced by further groups which settled at sites such as Abingdon, where the River Ock rejoined the Thames; and the other Thames-side concentration of settlement, Eynsham. Yet others travelled up the Ock to Frilford. Occupying former Roman sites; these groups at Abingdon and Frilford were in small numbers but able to dominate the local people whose centuries of prosperous stability, albeit in servitude, had left them unfitted for aggressive confrontation, while plague and famine had devastated the country weakening or removing any resistance.

It is assumed that these first Anglo-Saxons were brought in initially in the early fifth century by the sub-Roman

42

authority from Old Saxony as German mercenaries to control these areas. Perhaps a British sub-Roman tyrant at Dorchester then began building a West Saxon kingdom for himself, as there was a rapid and early build-up in the Oxford region with an apparently deliberate placement of communities at strategic intervals. Such was at Frilford, at a site which controlled the upper reaches of the Ock and the north-south road, an important ceremonial gathering place with a small town covering 74 acres, boasting a Roman temple and a large amphitheatre almost 70 yards in diameter with a wall encircling the arena. Historians consider this and other sites are more relevant to a power-base at Dorchester than to any larger strategy of control.

The placing of a few armed men and their families at key localities was later extended to many other sites, continuing in the Oxford region into the second half of the fifth century. At the same time other Anglo-Saxons continued to arrive in the East Midlands and Sussex. The former were refugees from the west side of continental Saxony, the latter a second wave of immigration from the land between the rivers Oste and Elbe. By about 500 there were no more Anglo-Saxon immigrants to come, and mongrel bands made up a second generation of settlers from Sussex and elsewhere who colonised southern Wessex, Hampshire and Wiltshire, in the late fifth and sixth centuries.

According to the Chronicle, Vortigern, a powerful ruler in Kent and the southern parts of Britain, invited German warriors in to help subdue his northern foes who had caused trouble there since the Roman departure. But the mercenaries, once in, took advantage of the weak situation and seized control of parts of the country for themselves. Hengest and Horsa, two Jutish warriors, had been banished from their own land and so accepted the invitation, we may suppose, with alacrity. Hengest was granted the Isle of

Thanet for his services, but soon invited others of his countrymen to join him there where he could control access to the Thames, allegedly bringing in 3,000 mercenaries. This was the beginning of the fighting between Briton and Anglo-Saxon which lasted until the latter had conquered the greater part of the country, confining the Britons to Wales and the northern kingdom of Strathclyde-Cumbria.

There was nothing of the stuff of great battles in this. It was less of a conquest than infiltration followed by usurpation, although there were many small battles and sometimes "great slaughter" of Britons who tried to resist. But there is no record of a certain portion of landed property, or of rents or produce, regularly set aside as tribute for the conquerors, as was the custom in other Germanic states on the Continent. Those Anglo-Saxons who had not brought women with them, took British women, just as the chief Vortigern did with a daughter of Hengest. As inheritance of property was recognised only in the male line, men did not weaken their positions by this. Furthermore, Britons who remained appear to have preserved their previous rights as the laws of Ine (688-694) indicate there was no big difference with regard to the *wergild* (the worth of a man according to his rank paid as a fine or compensation by the man who slew him); the capability of bearing witness; and other rights between Britons and Anglo-Saxons.

But former Roman towns now became deserted ruins as it became the turn of the Britons to emigrate, particularly the more affluent villa owners. Many left in the middle of the fifth century for Brittany to which they gave their name. Others retreated to fortified positions so a certain amount of conflict must have taken place. But evidence of wholesale massacres as reported by Gildas, a sixth century monk who wrote "The Ruin of Britain" and who considered that the

Britons deserved their fate to be "slaughtered in heaps" or forced into emigration because of their sinful behaviour, is wanting. Gildas's condemnation, written just before 547 and about a century after the events had taken place, was largely copied in 731 by Bede, a monk of Wearmouth and Jarrow, in his "The Ecclesiastical History of the English Nation". Only on the Isle of Wight was Caedwalla alleged to have exterminated all of the inhabitants.

The Devastated Land

The effective control exercised by these small numbers of Anglo-Saxons who led detachments of Britons as their troops, was no more remarkable than that practised over vast areas and vastly superior numbers by European colonial administrations in countries such as Africa in modern colonial times. It is only necessary to remove the leaders of dissension and revolt and the vast majority of people submits to the new authority. The mystery is the sudden abandonment of late Roman rural sites before the middle of the fifth century; equally where no Saxons were evident, as at Appleford, and two centuries later at Ducklington, both Oxfordshire Thames-side villages.

Gildas, wrong in many things, may have been correct when he wrote of famine and a great plague preceding the arrival of the Anglo-Saxons. By the time that they came, Britain had already ceased to be Roman, but it was plague which may have spelt the end of Roman Britain. Not necessarily the "Black Death", but influenza, typhoid, or some other contagious disease. Plague ravaged the western Mediterranean in the early 440s, the period when refugees

45

were fleeing Britain, so perhaps it was carried there from Britain. The Britain that the first Anglo-Saxon settlers found was a land in distress, with homes empty and the once rich cornfields lying fallow and untended for want of labour. Had it been otherwise, the Anglo-Saxons may have met with more resistance. As it was they saw an opportunity to seize lands which appeared to be abandoned. That these earliest Anglo-Saxons cremated their dead may have been a response to plague conditions.

By the end of the fifth century, or the beginning of the sixth, the Germanic population of the Upper Thames had stopped recruitment from overseas and had settled down to integrate with the surviving Romano-British inhabitants.

But these settlers had reverted to a level of material culture below that of their ancestors in the first century BC and below that subsequently found in Britain under the Romans. Under the stability of Roman rule many substantial buildings in stone and terracotta were erected, creating a class of British builders and other workmen which became in demand for restoring the deserted provinces on the Continent. Now the people had seemingly no tradition of building anything more substantial than timber houses. Neither invader nor invaded built new structures in stone with tiled roofs. British and English took the structures left by Iron Age and Roman communities and used them in their own more primitive ways. Just as they exploited at a greatly reduced level the formerly intensively managed landscape which they had taken over.

We know that the earliest Anglo-Saxons were thin on the ground and as much as anything this apparent apathy may have been due to a want of sufficient people, the native population which could have supplied slaves destroyed by plague and emigration; the situation then maintained by the strife of warring factions. A lack of aspiration to better things may not have resulted from a decline in intelligence or ability, for since the days of Ceawlin Wessex was engaged in constant warfare with its British and Anglo-Saxon neighbours, the country likened to a vast military camp. In the year 626 at least seven kings of the Gewisse are mentioned, more properly perhaps they should be called chiefs. Internecine strife between these rival chiefs, as well as Danish pillaging, meant that it was not possible to lead a settled life, to construct substantial buildings or to develop an agricultural economy. Stone buildings were easily located and attacked, but not so easy to re-build after they had been destroyed. Much easier, and less costly of time and effort, was to build timber and thatch structures. Little loss if they were burnt down and simple to rebuild somewhere else. Not until Alfred had brought some stability to the country did building in stone begin again.

Large cornfields were easily found and burnt or ravaged by enemies. So reduced, patchy agriculture, with a concentration on root crops, would have been demanded. Thus agriculture did not maintain the degree it had reached under the Roman occupation, although it improved considerably towards the end of the era as evinced by the numerous towns which developed and whose inmates had to be fed.

Although larger centres such as Abingdon existed, the early Anglo-Saxon landscape in the Oxford region for the most part seems to have comprised varied small and mobile settlements, not centralised villages. A centralised village system only became evident in late Anglo-Saxon or post-Conquest times. This was brought about by a combination of greater political stability, increase in population and evolution of the communal open-field system of agriculture. In addition the establishment of the church parochial system where the church became the centre of a parish which surrounded it, and the institution of feudal authority in which the lord oversaw a community, completed the change.

Wessex had no natural defences other than the high ground of the Downs; but martial discipline, legitimate succession of leaders or kings, and a tranquil state of possession, were rendered so permanent in the country that it was able to adopt gradual improvements until one of its æthelings, Cynegils, united the descendants of the invading hordes into a closer connection and brought them into a higher degree of political culture.

Cynegils' baptism and his marriage to the daughter of Oswald, the king of Northumbia, would have given the Gewisse Northumbrian protection against the Mercians or 'boundary folk', the name adopted by the Anglo-Saxons occupying the swathe of country from the lower Trent to the forests of the western Midlands. But this alliance collapsed in 642 when Oswald, known as "the fair or free of hand" by friend and foe alike, was killed in battle by Penda, the ruthless Mercian king whose sister had married Cenwealh of Wessex. But Cenwealh then made the mistake of casting her aside and Penda, to avenge his sister, drove the Gewissian king into exile for three years with Anna, the king of the East Angles.

The Strife Begins

Penda now had an excuse to go to war with Anna, a war in which Anna was killed. Penda then obliged Anna's brother and successor, Æthelhere, to go to war with him against Oswiu, whose brother Oswald Penda had slain. Oswiu, a devout Christian, attempted to treat with Penda, but the latter marched against him with the announced intention of exterminating the entire nation of the Northumbrians. Oswiu vowed that if he, Oswiu, was victorious, then he would give twelve estates for the erection of cloisters and dedicate his twelve-month old daughter Ælflæd to perpetual virginity and a monastic life. Fortunately for the Northumbrians, but perhaps unfortunately for little Ælflæd, Penda was killed in the ensuing battle together with nearly all of his chieftains, many of the soldiers being drowned in the river Are which had overflowed its banks. Oswiu ceded South Mercia to Peada, the eldest son of Penda, murdered the following year by the treachery of his wife. Oswiu now ruled the whole of Mercia as a Christian king until two years later he was forced out by the revolt of three ealdormen.

Wulfhere, a younger son of Penda, who had fled into hiding on the death of his father, now appeared and took over the throne of Mercia in 656 and soon resumed the expansionist campaigns of his father. In 661 he "harried on Ashdown" and had obviously ravaged across the Vale throwing the political authority south of the Thames into disarray. The Gewissian kings and their bishops found the Upper Thames too hot for them and decamped to Winchester, abandoning the see of Dorchester. Thus had it not been for Wulfhere, Dorchester might have become the capital of England. As it was, it remained the gateway to the Thames, leading from land-locked Mercia to London and thus to northern Europe.

Anglo-Saxon kings were bent on military dominance and the annexation of tribute, not on ethnic displacement to create space for their own people. Hence the people of the Upper Thames now owed their food tribute or their military service to a Mercian chief, not to the king of the Gewisse.

49

The Trusties

The Upper Thames leaders had called themselves the Gewisse according to the generally reliable chronicle of Bede, which may have been a self-imposed nickname for a strong-arm gang, perhaps meaning "the Trusties". Birinus had referred to them as "utter pagans", choosing to work first among them to convert to Christianity. Egbert later (825) styled himself "rex Gewissorum" but the Gewisse were not the dignified kingly lineage that Alfred liked to imagine.

Although the Gewisse may have ventured into the Vale on raiding exploits, we do not really know who occupied this area at the foot of the Downs at this time. Their paganism and the undoubted association of White Horse Hill and its environs with pagan beliefs suggests however that they would probably have been the occupants, for it is the only area so strongly associated with parallels in their beliefs. Britain had not been an entirely pagan country upon their arrival, churches had already begun to appear in Wessex in late Roman times, at least farther west, Christianity coming to the lowlands of Britain by the late third or early fourth century. The Roman Empire was officially Christian from the 360s, and the public practice of paganism was banned from 391.

But for now, in the middle of the seventh century, the Gewissian king and his armies were obliged to move out and were more successful on the south coast. In the latter half of the seventh century they gained control of those Hampshire lands which the late ninth century chronicler writing in the Anglo-Saxon Chronicle claimed as their original homelands.

Ceadwalla, "a most vigorous youth of the royal race of the Gewisse", exiled from the Upper Thames area, killed

King Æthelwealh of Sussex, wasting Sussex and Kent with a savage slaughter and devastation before he was driven out. In 685 he became king of the Gewisse, and then attacked Sussex and Kent again, killing one of the ealdormen who had driven him out before, and once more reducing the country to a "grievous servitude" ruling it "with a rod of iron". But then he suddenly repented. Abdicating in 688 he went to Rome to be baptized. He was apparently replaced as king of the West Saxons by Coenred, supported by his son Ine who probably acted as an underking ruling Sussex. Coenred, perhaps too old or suffering ill-health, appears to have been succeeded as king by Ine after four or five years, then becoming his son's supporter in office. Ine, with his aggressive and headstrong character, may not have given his father any option.

The seventh-century kings passed not their time in grand palaces but were always on the move, circuiting with their retinues around their scattered royal vills, living off the food tribute provided by each. The bigger the kingdom, the more extensive the circuit, but in the largest areas the king occupied a core area and the surrounds were controlled by deputies or sub-kings. Some vills acquired long-term permanence, such as Benson, first mentioned in 571 and still the most valuable royal manor in Oxfordshire in 1086. In the early 670s there was a sub-king at Thame, a place also still important in 1086.

Ine became one of the best known of these early kings because of his laws, which Alfred later used. But Ine, in spite of his wise laws, in the preamble to which he acknowledges the help of his father, was as much a tyrant as the other kings. We do not begin to hear of his exploits until five years after his succession, when he avenged himself on the people of Kent for the murder of his kinsman Mul, for which the Kentish king paid a wergeld of thirty thousand pounds. Expelling the nobility from the country, Ine was not satisfied until he had ravaged East Anglia. He also fought with the Britons, in one battle putting to flight the British prince Geraint. In 715 he fought against the Mercians in a memorable battle at Wenborough in Wiltshire.

Yet this fierce king's friend and counsellor was a bishop, Aldhelm, who was also known as a great Latin poet. Under his influence Ine founded and endowed monasteries, re-building and enlarging the old Abbey of Glastonbury. But he is best remembered for the seventy-six laws of Wessex which he collected together. In them, baptism of a child within thirty days was compulsory, but they also specially referred to theft, murder or manslaughter, feuds and mone-tary compensation; with others applicable to the British subjects who were placed on an almost equal footing. But he also introduced the first laws covering conservation and agriculture.

Concerned already at the end of the seventh century at the loss of woodland, Ine was responsible for the first con-servation law, forbidding the felling and burning of trees; evidence of clearing for agriculture by the slash and burn technique. But the value of trees was probably seen in providing pannage, timber for ship and other building, fuel, and charcoal for iron-smelting and pottery-making. Woods also had an important role to play in strategic warfare, providing cover in which to hide from an enemy or to ambush him from. But much of the value of woodland consisted in the oak and beech mast which supplied food (pannage) for the numerous herds of swine which were reared. The worth of a tree was reckoned according to the number of swine which could stand under it. Thus if anyone cut down a tree under which 30 swine could stand, a pretty small tree, he was liable to the full fine of sixty shillings, as was someone who burned a tree in a wood "because fire is a thief", presumably meaning that the tree could have been used as fuel. If someone felled many trees in a wood, then the fine was thirty shillings for each of the first three trees. Woodland was also valued for hunting as wild animals were an important source of food, especially in the winter. Hunting was the chief recreation of the highest personages, both temporal and ecclesiastical.

In the fens the people drained swamps and built embankments, bringing new areas into cultivation. But the chief occupation of the Anglo-Saxons was the rearing of cattle. Every husbandman or farmer received, on being settled on the land of his lord, seven sown acres on his yard of land, two oxen, a cow, and six sheep. The cattle of the free tenants were driven with those of the lord to graze on the common pasture. A law forbade the shearing of sheep before midsummer, wool being the principle article of export. Swine rearing was followed wherever the old oak and beech woods still existed. Many horses were bred, every man being obliged to have two for his plough, and they were also exported, for a later law of Athelstan (circa 930) was to forbid this, the Danes appreciating their value for use in war.

Agriculture seems to have been adequate as there is no record of export or import of grain; and those recorded instances of famine and disease are less than for other contemporary nations. William of Poitiers in 1071 was to call England a store-house of Ceres (the Roman grain goddess), from its abundance of grain. Under the laws of Ine the greater part of the larger landed possessions had to be kept under cultivation. Orchards also became frequently mentioned at the end of the era, distinct from the vineyards attached to almost every monastery.

Murder and Counter Murder

The latter years of Ine's reign were less prosperous than most of the earlier ones. He slew the ætheling Cynewulf, who was probably plotting rebellion for Cynewulf's followers afterwards seized Taunton, a town built by Ine. Ine carried on a war against Sussex, and others in Cornwall and Glamorgan. Ealdbert, another ætheling, fled Wessex after the loss of Taunton, wandering in exile in Surrey until he was found and slain by Ine. The following year, after 37 years as king, Ine resolved to abdicate following the example of his predecessor Ceadwalla, and pass the remainder of his life in Rome in devotion.

Ine was succeeded by his kinsman Æthelheard, who held the throne for fourteen years until his death in 741. Cuthred then succeeded and resolutely made war against Æthelbald, who had succeeded to the throne of Mercia in 716.

The battle for the Mercian Cotswold centre of Burford in 752 led by Cuthred, was to the West Saxons a struggle for life and liberty, to the Mercians for supremacy in Britain. Victory for the West Saxons freed Wessex from all further aggression on the part of other Anglo-Saxon states, and from that time on the dynasty rapidly rose to supremacy over all the others, a supremacy which was to be maintained for three centuries. Victory was allegedly due to the valour of Æthelhun who, bearing the banner of the golden dragon of Wessex, marched forward and slew the Mercian standard-bearer. After a vigorous battle the Mercians, under their leader Æthelbald, suddenly turned tail and fled. Two years before Cuthred had fought with the "arrogant ealdorman" Æthelhun, who presumably had now acknowledged Cuthred as his king.

The year after the victory at Burford, Cuthred fought the

Britons but presumably the outcome was not successful as no record of the result is reported. In 756, the year in which Canterbury was burned down, he died, and his kinsman Sigeberht who descended from the Kentish kings, became king of the West Saxons. But Cynewulf and the councillors of Wessex deposed him "for unlawful actions" leaving him with Hampshire only, while Cynewulf, literally "royal wolf", ruled the rest. But Sigeberht slew the ealdorman Cumbra, who had been faithful to him throughout. This was considered to be such a crime that Cynewulf drove him away and he fled to the Weald. Here he lived until near a stream at Privett, he was ignominiously stabbed to death by a herdsman, perhaps in the hope of a royal reward.

In this same year (756) Æthelbald, king of Mercia, was murdered at Seckington. He was succeeded by Beornred who was replaced in the same year by Offa, son of Thingferth, who was to rule Mercia for 39 years. Significant as Offa's reign was to prove to be, the defeat of the Mercians at Burford had marked the beginning of Mercian decline.

The first Offa or Uffo was the son of Waermund, king of Angeln, allegedly blind from birth until his seventh year and dumb until his thirtieth, but who suddenly recovered his speech and sight when war threatened. Offa the son of Thingferth was so named because he also was allegedly dumb, blind and lame from birth. But like his ancestor he allegedly acquired speech, sight, and "fleetness of foot", when his country was attacked. In 777 he beat Cynewulf at Benson, an Anglo-Saxon royal palace, and captured it. Another tyrant king, in 794 he had Ethelbert, King of East Anglia, beheaded. A king afterwards recognised as a saint.

Cynewulf meanwhile "fought great battles against the Welsh", but he wished to expel an ætheling called Cyneheard, brother of Sigeberht. In 786 Cyneheard, knowing the king's intentions towards him, and learning that he was visting a mistress at Meretun, surrounded the chamber with his men, taking the king and his men by surprise. Coming to the doorway the king defended himself and then, catching sight of Cyneheard, rushed out and wounded him, whereupon a furious fight ensued in which the king was killed. It appears that the king's love-nest was some distance from the lodgings of his thegns, for they did not come to the rescue until they heard the woman screaming after the king was dead. Cyneheard tried to treat with the king's thegns, offering them money and their lives, but to their great honour they would not hear of it. All fought to the death except for one British hostage who was severely wounded.

Cyneheard then fortified himself inside the building with his men, where he was still the next day when reinforcements arrived to aid Cynewulf's men upon hearing that the king had been slain. When two ealdormen Osric and Wigfrith approached the gate, Cyneheard offered them money and land if they would acknowledge him as king. Refusing his offer, the dead king's men attacked the gates and smashed their way in, killing Cyneheard and all of the men who were with him, except for one who was the godson of one of the ealdormen.

The Coming of the First Danes

Beorhtric, who claimed direct descendancy from Cerdic, succeeded to the West Saxon kingdom after Cynewulf's death, ruling until 802. He had been chosen by the witan as king in preference to Ealhmund, King of Kent, who was next in the line of succession. It was during his reign, in 789, that the landing of the first Danes took place with its grim consequences.

On being informed that three ships had landed on the coast of Dorset, perhaps an unintentional landing due to wind or weather, the king's reeve Beaduheard, who resided at Dorchester a considerable distance inland, supposing them to be smugglers rode to the spot and ordered them to be secured and taken to the king. Whereupon he was attacked by the Danes and he and all of his retinue killed.

According to the fifteenth-century chronicle known as John of Brompton's, although it is not known who wrote it or where, a Dane of royal birth, Ragnar Lothbrok, was shipwrecked on the coast of Norfolk and befriended by King Edmund. As a result of this friendship he was murdered by the king's huntsman through jealousy of Lothbrok's hunting skills. Lothbrok's sons, Inguar and Hubba, hearing that their father had been slain by Edmund, who knew nothing of his huntsman's involvement, swore vengeance upon the king, and so began the long series of bloody battles between Anglo-Saxon and Dane which ravaged Britain for the next two centuries. Battles for power, not the skirmishes with roaming bandits which had begun in the eighth century.

But these explanations are regarded merely as romances, and the real reason behind the Danish attacks was simply that they could pillage without opposition a country rich in cattle and agricultural produce. They concentrated on attacking the two kingdoms, Wessex and Mercia, which were least able to make a defence.

Upon the death of Beorhtric, Egbert, who had been driven to France by the combined efforts of Offa and Beorhtric in 789, succeeded to the kingdom. Beorhtric had helped Offa because the latter had married his daughter.

Now, in an attempt to seize power before Egbert returned from France, Ealdorman Æthelmund rode from the province of the Hwiccians across the Thames at Kempsford, but was confronted by Ealdorman Weohstan and an army from Wiltshire. Both ealdormen were killed in the ensuing battle, but the Wiltshire men won the day, keeping the West Saxon kingdom intact.

We hear nothing more of Egbert until 815, when he ravaged Cornwall from east to west. Ten years later he revenged himself on the Mercians when he fought them at Ellendun or Wroughton, winning with a great slaughter. Encouraged by this, he sent his son Æthelwulf to drive King Bealdred of Kent north across the Thames. The people of Kent and Surrey, together with the South and East Saxons, then submitted to him. Later in the same year the king of the East Angles and his people appealed to Egbert for protection against the Mercians, although they themselves succeeded in killing Beornwulf, the Mercian king. Ludeca, who succeeded Beornwulf, only lasted for two years before he was also killed in internal squabbles, and Wiglaf succeeded to the kingdom.

Two years after Wiglaf's accession Egbert conquered the kingdom of the Mercians and everything south of the Humber, becoming the eighth king to be called 'Bretwalda' or 'mighty ruler'. After this victory he then proceeded against the Northumbrians who submitted to him without a fight. But it seems that the following year Wiglaf got back the kingdom of Mercia while Egbert was fighting the Welsh into submission. Then in 836 Egbert found himself confronting a different enemy, and was defeated by a Danish seafaring party at Carhampton.

Two years later a great Danish naval force arrived and joined forces with the West Welsh to fight Egbert. Egbert confronted them at Hingston Down, putting both Welsh

58

and Danes to flight. The following year Egbert died and was succeeded by his son Æthelwulf. Æthelwulf gave his eldest son, Æthelstan, control of Kent, the East Saxons, Surrey and the South Saxons. Perhaps he had seen the dangers of trying to spread himself too thinly, for his reign was to mark the beginning of a determined effort by the Danes to conquer the country.

ALFRED THE GREAT A.D.871-A.D.901 CT GLEICHEN, SCULPT

Chapter 3

The King Alfred Legend

The Battles for Survival

I am that oft-defeated King
Whose failure fills the land,
Who fled before the Danes of old,
Who chaffered with the Danes for gold,
Who now upon the Wessex Wold
Hardly has feet to stand.
              G.K.Chesterton. 1911.

From Pagan Belief to Christian Ethic

Emergent of those bloody mists of time, nowhere else of all
the Germanic peoples have so many memorials of paganism been preserved as among the Anglo-Saxons, despite
the purging of pagan beliefs by Christianity. These survivals are due in part to Pope Gregory's instruction in 601
to the leader of the second group of missionaries to
England, Mellitus, to tell Augustine, the first Christian
missionary who had arrived on the Isle of Wight in 597, not
to destroy the pagan temples, only their idols. The temples
themselves were to be purified and adapted to the Christian
religion. Sacrifices of animals could continue but to
provide feasting for Christian festivals. By incorporating
the pagan customs into the Christian religion, conversion
was less likely to meet with opposition. However Gregory
was less compromising in his instructions to the newly-bap-
tised Kentish king Æthelbert, whom he urged to destroy the

temple buildings. But a result of the policy of avoiding outright confrontation is that we still call the days of the week after the names of the heathen gods, although the association is fortuitous. Tuesday after Tiw the god who presided over the formalities of war and law; Wednesday surprisingly retained after Woden the one-eyed chief of the gods; Thursday after Thor the red-bearded giant of strength; and Friday after Frigg, the northern counterpart of Venus, wife of Woden. While Saturday, Sunday and Monday, are named, as the Saxons named them, after the planets Seterne, Sun and Moon. The most important Christian festival, Easter, was named after the pagan goddess Eostre.

Pagan worship was still remembered in the tenth century, for a boundary description of Abingdon refers to "the foul oak" *(Fulan Aec)* on its northern boundary, which may have referred to pagan tree worship connected with the cult of Woden, its memory still preserved by a small plantation called Blake's Oak. Another translation simply gives it as "diseased oak", but there is surely no disease of an oak tree which could merit such a description (1). Dead, decayed or sick, maybe; but not foul or dirty, and the modern survival Blake's Oak probably derives from *blaec aec* or 'the black oak'.

Before conversion to the Christian faith, Anglo-Saxon men knew no greater disgrace than to die in bed and some had themselves speared to death to avoid this dreadful ignominy. But the longing after the cowl, as the German historian Lappenberg aptly expressed it, replaced the use of the harness, and this pagan Anglo-Saxon trait was to be transferred into what is known today as the "Christian work ethic". We still regard it as glorious to die on the battle field. After all, few would want to fight if it were not.

The Danes Secure a Foothold

After Æthelwulf ascended the throne, hardly a year seemed to pass without a battle somewhere or other against the Danes. In 851 they wintered in England for the first time on the Isle of Thanet, and in 855 on the Isle of Sheppey, the beginning of their foothold. Æthelwulf obviously did not consider that this posed any great threat for he took himself off to Rome for a year. On the way home he married the child bride Judith, daughter of Charles the Bald, king of the Franks. His new-found nuptial bliss was short-lived for he died two years later in 860. During this time we hear nothing of the Danes who must have been either trying to establish a peaceful foothold, or simply indulging in minor skirmishes.

The king's son Æthelbald now succeeded to Wessex, while Æthelbert became king of Kent, Essex, Surrey and Sussex; Æthelstan having died some years before. Possibly shortly after Æthelbald's accession the Danes stormed Winchester, but were put to flight by the ealdormen Osric of Hampshire and Æthulwulf of Berkshire. The rest of Æthelbald's reign was apparently peaceful until his death five years later; but not so in Æthelbert's kingdom. In 865 a party of Danes camped on the Isle of Thanet making peace with the people of Kent, who promised the invaders money if they would but observe the pact. But, "like foxes", as one chronicler puts it, the enemy stole away during the night and ravaged the whole of eastern Kent.

With the death of his brother Æthelbald, Æthelbert now succeeded to the entire kingdom of the West Saxons. He seemingly had five years' uneventful reign after which he too died and his body was buried in Sherborne Minster.

The year was now 866 and Alfred, younger brother to the successor to the crown, Æthelred, was eighteen. We may wonder why the Danes had apparently been so quiet during the past ten years, but it seems that there was not enough of them to pose any real threat. Little more than bands of brigands, they contented themselves with trying to exploit any period of possible political instability which might ensue after a ruler's death before the successor could achieve firm control. But in the autumn of that year a great army of Danes landed in East Anglia, this time not a band of skirmishing pirates as had frequently harried the coastal regions, but an army determined to conquer. Unwilling to confront such a force, the East Anglians bought them off and provided them with horses; leaving them to attack the Northumbrians and storm the town of York.

Alfred's Battles Begin

The West Saxons were not involved in the battles until 868 when the Danes took up winter quarters in Nottingham, and Burgred, king of Mercia, requested Æthelred's help. Burgred was able to do this because in 853 he had married Æthelwulf's daughter Æthelswyth, sister of Æthelred and Alfred, cementing a close alliance between the two kingdoms. Now the Mercian queen's two brothers marched to Nottingham without delay and with Burgred besieged the town but could not take it. So Burgred made peace with them and the West Saxons returned home, leaving the Danes to winter at Nottingham.

The Danes spent the following year at York and then apparently received large reinforcements headed by kings Baegseeg and Halfdene. Thus strengthened, in 870 they marched openly across Mercia into East Anglia and took up winter headquarters at Thetford. Here they were attacked

64

by King Edmund whom they succeded in wounding and capturing. Allegedly tying him to a tree they executed him with arrows in retaliation for his supposed complicity in the death of Ragnar. But such vengeance alone was not enough for the barbarous brothers Inguar and Hubba, who now began to pillage and conquer far and wide in a mad frenzy of hate.

The whole of north and east of England was left a desolate wilderness behind the invaders. London was in ruins and Kent had been repeatedly ravished. But some thirty miles up the Thames was a fair kingdom stretching far to the west. This was Wessex, kingdom of the West Saxons, ruled over by Æthelred, the brother of Alfred. Peace had reigned for ten years and the land was prospering.

At the end of 870 Inguar and Hubba suddenly sailed up the Thames with their troops and seized Reading, a royal fortified town at that time the easternmost town of note in Wessex. Camped where Reading railway station now stands, the Danes began to ravage the countryside far and wide. The West Saxons were taken by surprise. They were not prepared so early in the year for the winter was not yet over. Æthelwulf, the Mercian ealdorman of Berkshire, gathered a small band together and "raged as a lion in battle", attacking the invaders at Englefield and putting them to flight.

Four days after this Æthelred, accompanied by his brother Alfred, came up from the west to support Æthelwulf's attack on the Reading fortifications which the Danes had constructed. But while Æthelred and his brother were setting up camp on the plain after an unsuccessful assault on the fortified position, the Danes suddenly rushed out at them, "like wolves they burst out of all the gates and joined battle with all their might", and the West Saxons, after a furious battle in which Æthelwulf was slain, were forced to retreat. Æthelred and Alfred were pursued as far as Wichelet (Whistley) Green about five miles to the east of Reading, but allegedly saved themselves by crossing the Thames at Twyford, less than a mile to the north at a ford which was unknown to the Danes. A logical enough course of events if the Danes had cut off their retreat westwards, the way they had come. Having crossed the Thames the defeated army made its way back westwards apparently still pursued by the enemy, but not before stealthily recovering the body of Æthelwulf from the battlefield. Such a hazardous procedure for an army in retreat probably related more to a lingering pagan belief in ensuring an afterlife for the deceased than esteem for Æthelwulf as a man.

The Great Battle of Ashdown

Four days later, on January the 8th, the brothers mustered all the forces that they could find and stood their ground at the famous battle of Ashdown. The engagement has often been related. The Danes divided into two companies, one commanded by the two Danish kings, Baegseeg and Halfdene, the other by their earls. The West Saxons copied the Danish tactics, also dividing into two companies. At dawn the Danes had taken possession of a piece of high ground crowned with short thick brushwood from which they showered the West Saxons with arrows as the latter tried to storm the hill.

According to Pauli, old German custom behoved King Æthelred to lead against generals of like rank, while Alfred the prince should have engaged the lesser division. But tradition has it that Alfred arrived early in the morning at the foot of the hill while Æthelred was still in his tent observing mass, declaring that until the priest had finished no human work would tear him away from fulfilling his duty towards God. It has been pointed out that the story of the devout man who refuses to leave his Mass even while under threat of attack, is identical with that in the Life of Count Gerald, a continental holy man, and its application to Æthelred is undoubtedly apocryphal (2). It has never been questioned why Alfred, allegedly so pious, went to the battleground rather than observe mass with his brother. It implies that Alfred had no faith in prayer. His answer was to go out and confront the enemy. However rash in retrospect, his surprise tactic undoubtedly distracted the enemy, making them unprepared to withstand the second wave of attack brought forward by the king, and what could have been a disaster for England turned out to Alfred's everlasting glory.

Pressed by the enemy and waiting in vain for Æthelred to appear, Alfred finally ordered an attack, usurping the king's authority. With his troops he rushed up the hill under the deadly hail of the arrows of his opponents, clashing in fierce hand to hand combat. But now, unperturbed by the tumult and fortified by his belief in God's help, Æthelred calmly appeared and took the lead. Carrying out the pre-arranged plan he opposed Baegseeg and Halfdene, slaying Baegseeg himself. Many Danish nobles also fell: earl Sidroc the Old, earl Sidroc the Younger, earl Osbern, earl Faena and King Harold. It is unlikely that "many thousands" of Danes were slain as the chroniclers would have us believe, but we can believe that the bodies of a few hundred were scattered far and wide "over the whole broad expanse of Ashdown", until the Danes wavered and fled across the Downs. The honours, it seems, should have gone to Æthelred, but it was Alfred who was to receive credit as the victor.

According to the tenth-century chronicler Æthelweard, a West Saxon ealdorman who translated the Anglo-Saxon Chronicle into Latin adding a number of embellishments of his own, from the time the Anglo-Saxons had first landed in Britain never was such a battle known. Elated with their success, the victors pursued the fleeing enemy throughout the night and the following day back to Reading, mercilessly cutting down the stragglers. For the first time since the battle of Aclea in 851 when Æthelwulf had been victorious, the Danes had sustained a complete defeat at the hands of the West Saxons. Alfred gained his reputation as the saviour of England from this battle, but this was by his own crafty manipulation of records of the event (3).

The actual site where the West Saxons stood and fought the battle of Ashdown has always been the subject of speculation, and one of the most recent analyses favours Kingstanding Hill on the Icknield Way at the eastern end of the Downs, just west of the ford over the Thames at Moulsford and not far from the villages of Aston, Aston Upthorpe and Aston Tirrold, Aston having been suggested to be the site by seventeenth century antiquaries. But Aston would have been rendered in Old English as East-tun or Easton. "Asser", writing a hundred years later, probably invented the story that the spot was marked by "a rather small and solitary thorn-tree which grew there", but the Hundred of Compton in which Kingstanding Hill lies was anciently known as the Hundred of Nachededorn, or "naked thorn". However, Ashbury terriers, records of land of Glastonbury Abbey of the thirteenth and sixteenth centuries, list six places ending in "thorn", among which are Barethorne and Stubbethorne. Both fit "Asser's" description just as well as Nachededorne, so the alleged thorn tree cannot be used to support such a claim (4).

68

It is logical that the fleeing West Saxons crossed back over the Thames at Moulsford after their defeat at Reading and stood at bay as soon as they reached the first piece of high ground. But like many others before me, I prefer to think of Ashdown near Ashbury and White Horse Hill as the probable site of the great battle. The West Saxons' first instinct would perhaps have been to retreat to Wantage, intending to use the old Iron Age defences, standing at the fort at Segsbury Down. But finding themselves hotly pursued they would not have wanted to bring the enemy onto the royal residence at Wantage and so veered west, standing at Ashdown above Ashbury. Perhaps also it was of paramount importance to them to defend the White Horse, a site which their Christian beliefs would no longer allow them to regard as sacred, but perhaps still revered as a memorial to their ancestry from Woden. A strong argument for near Ashbury as the site has recently been made, based upon references in the Ashbury terriers to a strip of un-cultivated land anciently called the Wayte, an Old English word which can be translated as an ambush, and it is suggested that the West Saxons ambushed the Danes here. Added to this a boundary point in a charter for Ashbury of 947 is termed *Rammesburi*, which could commemorate ravens haunting the place of those which died in the battle. There is also the neighbouring locality to Ashbury of Kingston Winslow, which has no known royal connection but may mean "the king's farm with the cliff where the enemy were turned round."

Wherever the battle was fought, the year 871 became a year for Berkshire men to be proud of as Thomas Hughes puts it, the stand at Ashdown probably saving England from domination by the pagan Danes. Of course Alfred himself and his bold Berkshire warriors had descended from nothing more than a band of German mercenaries little different to the Danes themselves, but victory by the Danes would have put the clock back four centuries.

Yet the battle was not a decisive one which would drive the Danes out of the country. They simply retreated to lick their wounds at the fortification which they had built at Reading, where either Halfdene was joined by another army or his losses at Ashdown were greatly exaggerated. For within two weeks we find the Danish king undaunted, taking on the West Saxons again at Basing (near Basingstoke), a day's march south of Reading, and beating them. Two months later the armies met again, this time at Meretun, and again the West Saxons were beaten.

It has been asked, why was the next battle south of Reading? But it seems logical that Æthelred tried to follow up the advantage he had gained at Ashdown by surprising the enemy from the rear, hence making a wide detour to the south. Unfortunately it seems he was surprised by a foraging or scouting party. That he was beaten may have been due to the fact that he only took a relatively small force with him to try and move undetected, and he perhaps underestimated the enemy's determination.

The Sack of Abingdon

There has been much speculation as to the site of Meretun, and among several sites which have been argued for, one recent proposal has been Marten on the Inkpen Ridgeway, adjoining Tidcomb to the west of Newbury; the assumption being that the Danes were intent upon attacking Winchester. But another possibility is that they were moving up the Thames to sack the monastery at Abingdon and were circumventing Wallingford when they were intercepted at Moreton west of Wallingford, the battle perhaps taking place on Cholsey Hill. For reasons which we shall never know, but probably because they would have discredited Alfred's image, the events are scantily recorded and the Anglo-Saxon Chronicler does not refer to the Danes' sacking of Abingdon which took place at this time. Only the errant chronicle of John of Brompton mentions the latter, and the chronicles of Abingdon Abbey themselves:

"O quis dolor et quae anxietas, et quis tam durae cervicis, tam ferrei pectoris, tam adamantini cordis, ut haec audiat et se a lachrimis abstineat?" lamented a monk of Abingdon. "Oh what sadness and what anxiety, and what man has such a hard neck, such a chest of iron, such adamantine sinews, that when he hears this holds back tears?"

A specific year for this sacking is not given, but the monks were forewarned, perhaps by the battle near Wallingford if such was where it took place, and fled to safety with their charters and relics. An angry chronicler records that the "satellites of Satan" had profaned holy ground, ferocious like lions and filled with detestable greed they had occupied the monastery until Christ himself drove them out. While the Danes were feasting in the abbey refectory, the image of Christ on the crucifix hanging on the wall stretched out His hand and hurled a stone into their midst (more likely the place began to fall down as a result of the attack upon it), whereupon the panic-stricken Danes fled, but not before they had set fire to the church.

It seems unlikely that the Danes were sufficiently numerous to risk sending out small raiding detachments so far from their base at Reading, especially after their experience at Ashdown, and that they must have been marching or sailing up the Thames rather than moving

71

westwards over the Downs. But after the battle of Meretun the Reading garrison was reinforced by "a great summer army", and the Danes now posed an even more malignant threat.

Alfred the King

Further misfortune to confront the West Saxons was that one month after the battle of Meretun Æthelred died and Alfred, at the age of 23, was now on his own, king of the West Saxons. Despite what we were led to believe by the inventions of "Asser" that Alfred had been chosen by his father as a child to succeed him, he probably had not expected to become king, certainly not so precipitately, and how he managed to win over the support of the *witan* in his election we do not know, for what struggles for the succession may have taken place are suppressed by the Chronicle. Under the law of succession of father to son Æthelred's eldest son Æthelwald should have succeeded to the crown, but he was still a child and Æthelwulf in his will had stated that his three sons should succeed to the exclusion of the children of any one of them, a provision that we may suppose was accepted by the *Witenagemot*. Thus the entire inheritance and the crown passed to Alfred. There was no recorded meeting of the *witan* to confirm his accession and we learn of no ceremony attaching to his coronation. Perhaps in the midst of warfare, with Guthrum and Inguar hungrily waiting in their fortified camp at the confluence of the Thames and the Kennet, and fresh bands constantly sailing up the Thames to join them, there was no time for strict adherence to the letter of the constitution.

 Æthelred perhaps died from wounds received in the

battle of Meretun. His body was laid to rest at Wimborne Minster after Easter, which in that year fell on the 15th of April. This location so far south, which Alfred probably chose because of his belief in his kingly lineage stemming from Hampshire, has been used to argue that the West Saxons were operating in this area, and that Meretun referred to Martin some 16 miles north of Wimborne. But one chronicler, Æthelweard, perhaps referring to Abingdon although no location is given, records that while Alfred was attending his brother's funeral a battle was lost by the smallness of the English force.

Whatever the strategy of the Danes, if indeed they had one, they did move westwards one month later to be met by Alfred, now king, at Wilton on the southern bank of the river Wylye just west of Salisbury, eventually to become the capital of Wessex. The Chronicle records that Alfred only had a small force with which he confronted the whole army, and although he fought far on into the day the Danes eventually won. This was the first of a whole series of setbacks suffered by Alfred as a military commander, inexperienced as he was to confront the threats which now pressed upon him.

Pauli suggests that during the month before the battle of Wilton, Alfred must have been residing in the western part of his kingdom before marching from Wimborne, but this seems unlikely for about this time a curious incident took place. The Abingdon Chronicles record that Alfred pillaged the monastery after it had already been ransacked by the Danes. If this was so, he may well have been residing at Wantage.

The Battles Continue

The Anglo-Saxon Chronicle tells us that in 871 nine general engagments were fought against the Danes south of the Thames. These were in addition to the expeditions which were not counted that Alfred, before he was king, and the ealdormen and thegns, often undertook by themselves. Æthelweard states that there were eleven battles.

After Wilton Alfred made peace with the enemy. It is not recorded that he bought them off, although this would be customary, the Danes demanding *Danegeld* which usually represented extremely high sums of money. Leaving Wessex the following year the Danes moved to London where it was the Mercians turn to treat with them. The following year they went into Northumbria and the Mercians there made peace with them again. But to no avail. Moving on to Repton they forced King Burgred to flee the country.

Burgred went to Rome where he eventually died. Conquering all of Mercia the Danes placed it in the hands of the English collaborator Ceolwulf II dismissed as "a foolish king's thegn", "a barbarian in cruelty." The attempt to belittle him may have been because he was perhaps the descendant of Ceolwulf I, deposed in 823, of ancient lineage he was the last king to rule Mercia independently before Egbert made it tributary. Thus the aim of the Danes may have been to humiliate the West Saxons by restoring in place of Burgred a rival from an ancient and prestigious royal line, a ruler who might also have the respect of the Mercian people. We see later that Ceolwulf acted as arbiter between great land-owners in his Mercian rule, performing the role expected of a sensible ruler.

The incidents of fighting must have been sporadic and relatively localised, for at this time the Pope wrote to the archbishops Æthelred of Canterbury and Wulfred of York instructing them that the clergy "throughout the land of England" should put off lay garments and resume the clerical vestments according to the custom of the Roman Church. They had taken to wearing tunics which, although voluminous, were too short, and should wear tunics reaching to the ankle. We could understand this if it were the nuns to whom he was referring, but perhaps the Pope's concern with dress at a time of such turmoil, instead of offering spiritual comfort, was that the monks should keep up standards in the face of adversity and not revert to a dress which was more in keeping with the Roman tunic.

In 875 the Danes pressed on with their conquests. Halfdene went with part of the army to the River Tyne and attacked the Picts and Strathclyde Britons. Two years later he was to be killed attacking Dublin. Three other kings, Guthrum, Oscetel and Anwend, went to Cambridge; while Alfred took on some at sea who were perhaps trying to surprise him from the south-west. Attacking seven ships he captured one and put the rest to flight.

A new assault on Wessex began the following year with the occupation of Wareham, the enemy army led by Guthrum "slipping past" the West Saxon army. But it is doubtful if Alfred gained the advantage of them as is alleged, when blockaded within the fort which they had occupied they eventually capitulated. His treaty with them was probably more to his disadvantage than theirs. Undertaking to leave Wessex by swearing to him on a sacred ring to keep the peace, which the Chronicle reports as an act of great fealty on their part which they had not done before for any nation, was probably customary. According to Æthelweard, Alfred paid them a sum of money to obtain these assurances and no doubt it was a cripplingly large sum.

75

Then suddenly, without regard for hostages which they had handed over and killing all of the Anglo-Saxon counterparts which Alfred had given them, they stole away by night westwards to Exeter instead of returning whence they had come. Learning of their treachery, Alfred hastily assembled a mounted band and galloped after them, but could not come up with the traitors before they had reached the safety of the fortress at Exeter.

Seemingly Guthrum had expected to be joined by a large fleet which set sail from the Wash in the New Year of 877, but this time fate was on Alfred's side, for when off Swanage the fleet was hit by a great storm and lost 120 ships with upward of 3,000 men. Guthrum's plan had now foundered and once more he treated with Alfred, swearing great oaths of fealty and giving him as many hostages as he wished. Then he retreated north to Gloucester in Mercia for the harvest.

Alfred's Defeat

Alfred now seemingly took his army to the royal estate at Chippenham in Wiltshire on the east bank of the Avon, but the next year (878) in midwinter immediately after the 6th of January, when the Anglo-Saxons would be recovering from merry-making after twelfth-night, Guthrum, assisted by another band recently arrived in South Wales, took them by surprise and succeeded in routing them. Overrunning Wessex Guthrum reduced the inhabitants to beggars, causing many to flee overseas and having at last achieved his aim of conquering Wessex, or most of it. Several pockets of resistance remained, and in particular one man did not submit. That man was Alfred, who managed to escape with a small band of followers.

Although the West Saxons had one success at Kynwith in Devonshire, Alfred was not with them and it appears that they were now disunited among themselves, for the Celts in the west were prone to ally themselves with the new invaders who were winning, mindful of the fact that the Anglo-Saxons had simply been another conqueror. The Anglo-Saxons themselves saw how their Anglian neighbours, because they had not resisted the invaders, still for the most part retained their old property and spoke their own language despite oppression. The Anglo-Saxons saw that resistance simply brought ruin upon themselves, and as Pauli puts it, "No command, no prayer, no entreaties of their once-beloved king, could move them to sacrifice their small possessions and their own personal safety for the preservation of the whole state." No one would now stand out to lead the people against the enemy. For ten years there had been almost continual fighting with the numbers of the enemy increasing all the while as that of the defenders continually decreased, Alfred could no longer place any reliance on many of his subjects, particularly those of British race. Many had fled overseas, while others preferred subjection to the Danes rather than continual strife, and rebelled against the king.

West Saxon power had suffered a sudden and complete collapse, the fall of Chippenham seemingly paralysing its forces. Alfred escaped into hiding in Selwood Forest and the marshes of Somerset along the river Parret with his wife and children. He was accompanied by Ethelnoth, ealdorman of the region, and a small band of followers consisting of a few nobles, warriors and vassals. Conducting a guerilla warfare, Alfred and his band sallied forth secretly and by night against the Danish invaders, and even against the local people to obtain food, who perhaps sometimes gave it willingly.

It is from this period that the story of Alfred burning the cakes arose, a story first met with about the end of the tenth century in the anonymous "Life of St. Neot". Alfred, so the story went, was one day sitting by the fire in the cow herd's hut where he had first sought shelter, preparing his bow and arrows, while the lady of the house, ignorant of his identity, busied herself baking bread. Seeing that the loaves on the hearth were beginning to burn, she ran and removed them, chiding the king, "Though you neglect to turn them when you see them burning, you are ready enough to eat them when hot."

A later folktale, the story appears nowhere else and bears all the marks of a popular theme in hagiographical invention, that of reversal of roles whereby the once powerful king has become a menial servant in a swineherd's hut.

Realising its impregnability by virtue of its situation, at Easter 878 (March 23rd) Alfred and his followers decided to come out of hiding and build a fortification on a small two-acre island which was surrounded by bogs and only accessible by boat. It became called Æthelinga-Eig or Athelney, the Prince's Island. Installed on his island he then began to be joined by his people, among the first to come to him being the nobles of Somerset with their followers. With their aid he conducted hit and run sorties against the Danes, retiring each time to his island fortification.

In the second week of May Alfred decided to make a break for it. The men of Devon under their ealdorman Odda had been under siege but made a sudden sally against their enemy, routing them and slaying the leader Hubba, the last of the Lothbrok brothers. This was the signal for Alfred to act and he moved to Brixton Deverill on the border between Somerset and Devon at a place called Egbert's Stone, supposed to be White Sheet Hill, close to a large

78

tumulus on the downs overlooking the Vale of Knoyle east of Selwood. From it you can command a view of Somerset "as nearly as far as the curvature of the earth allows", as one writer expressed it.

Here Alfred was joined by forces from Wiltshire and Hampshire and the army then moved north to near Warminster where they camped for the night. The following day they quickly marched on northwards towards Chippenham to be confronted by the enemy 14 miles before it at Ethandune (Edington), Guthrum evidently having been apprised of the attack.

The Decisive Battle

We are told little of this desperate battle except that Alfred's forces met the enemy in close order forming a shield-wall, and had to persevere resolutely for a long time before they were victorious and the enemy fled. Alfred and his men pursued them the 14 miles to the camp at Chippenham, slaying all of the fleeing enemy that they could lay their hands on. Arrived at the stronghold they seized the horses and cattle and everything else which was outside, and then laid siege to the enemy camp for two weeks until the defenders capitulated.

Again Alfred entered into a treaty with the enemy, although the deceitful Guthrum may not have been present. Only the enemy is referred to as giving Alfred as many distinguished hostages as he wished and swearing to leave his kingdom immediately, he giving no hostages in return. But before Alfred allowed them to depart northwards their king apparently promised that he would receive baptism. Three weeks later Alfred was in camp at Aller near

Athelney when Guthrum arrived with 29 of his officers to be baptized, Alfred giving him the Christian name of Æthelstan. Eight days later at Wedmore when the chrysmal fillet was unbound, the first West Saxon *Witenagemot* was held since the times of oppression had begun.

Alfred and Æthelstan, as Guthrum was now called, agreed on the division of East Anglia for Æthelstan, and Wessex with a part of Mercia for Alfred. After remaining twelve days with Alfred, Guthrum returned to his people loaded with costly gifts. Alfred, rather than being determined to charm his enemy, probably had no option but to buy him off yet once more.

Historians agree that this battle was the turning-point. In saving Wessex. Alfred had saved England for the second time from heathen Scandinavian domination, this time on his own. Under the treaty with Guthrum, which was a diplomatic achievement much more important than the battle itself, Alfred became established as king of the whole of England south of the Thames, recovering the provinces which had been absorbed into Wessex in the ninth century (Berkshire, Surrey, Sussex, Kent, Essex, parts of Hertfordshire and Bedfordshire); while Guthrum retained Oxfordshire, Buckinghamshire, Middlesex, the rest of Hertfordshire and Bedfordshire, in Mercia.

That Alfred regained so much territory indicates the powerful situation he had attained over the Danish army, which had to give up its new settlements around Gloucester. In addition Guthrum forfeited much of the kingdom which had been ruled by his people since the time of his grandfather.

Although agreement had been reached, there was still no guarantee that it would be honoured any more than the previous treaties had been, and indeed, Alfred's troubles were by no means over.

The Strife Continues

The next year the Danish army, which seems to have been at Chippenham, moved to Cirencester, and the following year to East Anglia where it "shared out the land". Another army camped at Fulham decided to transfer its adventuring to the Continent and moved to Ghent in the Frankish empire. But England was not left alone, for in 882 Alfred took on four Danish ships, capturing two of them and killing all of the crews; while two other crews surrendered after great losses. The following year we find that an English army is camped near London to contain the enemy. Then in 885 the Danish army on the continent separated into two, one part betaking itself across the Channel to Kent and besieging Rochester. The inhabitants managed to hold the city until Alfred arrived with reinforcements, taking the enemy by surprise. The Danes retreated to their ships, leaving behind horses which they had captured on the Continent. Some of them then returned across the sea, while others entered into a treaty yet once more with Alfred.

Those who remained then twice broke their treaty by raiding the country south of the Thames and then, receiving aid from the Danes settled in East Anglia, they proceeded to the north bank of the Thames and camped at Benfleet. From here they made raiding excursions into the surrounding country, supported by the East Anglian people. Alfred therefore sent a naval force to East Anglia which encountered 16 Danish ships in the mouth of the river Stour. Seizing the ships the Anglo-Saxons killed all of the men and proceeded to return home with their booty, suggesting that this was a punitive expedition sent by Alfred because the army there had broken the peace. But the expedition then encountered another large naval force of Danes which had been got together by those inhabiting East Anglia. This time the Danish force won. But Alfred soon re-established his authority in the region and would have driven Guthrum out if the latter had not had help from Rollo, the first duke of Normandy.

Generations have been mislead by "Asser" stating that in 886 Alfred, in a bid to completely expel the Danish army, attacked London with great force and occupied it after "the burning of cities and the massacre of people". Alfred's role was probably only supportive of his son-in-law the Mercian ealdorman Æthelred, who had married Alfred's daughter Æthelflæd. Æthelred's assumption of control of London, which had always been Mercian, may have been due to his greater superiority over Alfred in the area. The Mercian puppet-king Ceolwulf II had disappeared from the scene by 879 and we do not know whether he or another ruled Mercia in the intervening seven years. But during his earlier reign the two kingdoms had enjoyed a shared coinage, suggesting that Alfred was also tributary to the Danes and that both he and Ceolwulf were obliged to issue their coins under Danish control.

After the battle of London the Danes decided to leave England alone for a few years, occupying themselves with attacks on the Continent. It was not until 892, six years later, that another attack was made by a great army complete with horses which crossed from Boulogne in 250 ships, sailing up the estuary of the Lympyne in East Kent as far as the Weald. Four miles up the estuary they stormed a fortress which had no more than a few peasants in it as it was only half built. Just after this the viking leader Haesten sailed up the Thames with 80 ships and made himself a fortress at Milton Royal near Sittingbourne, while yet another army made a camp at Appledore in South Kent on the edge of the Romney Marshes.

The following year the Northumbrians and the East

Anglians swore oaths to Alfred, and the East Anglians handed over six preliminary hostages, presumably swearing that they would not side with the Danes. But the East Anglians always broke their oaths, joining with the raiders. Alfred then gathered his army together and took up a position between the camp near the Weald and that on the Thames. But the enemy only came out of their camps twice; first when they landed and before Alfred had assembled his army, and secondly when they wished to leave with their booty to carry it across the Thames into Essex to meet their ships. Instead of confronting Alfred as an army, they used small raiding parties which pillaged left and right. Alfred therefore divided his army into two, sending out half of it on counter offensives against the raiding parties, while the rest remained guarding the boroughs. After Easter the enemy raided as far west as Wessex, pillaging in Hampshire and Berkshire.

When they tried to reach the ships they were intercepted at Farnham by Alfred's son Edward, who was in charge of the eastern forces and who put them to flight recovering the booty. The Danes fled across the Thames and up along the river Colne seeking refuge on Thorney Island where Edward laid siege to them.

But Edward's division had completed its term of service and its provisions were used up, so Edward seemingly abandoned the siege and began to make his way home. Alfred therefore began to march to Thorney, the Danes remaining on the islet because their king was wounded and too ill to be moved. But those Danes who lived in Northumbria and East Anglia collected about 100 ships and went south around the coast to lay siege to Exeter; while another 40 ships went north and besieged a fortress on the north Devon coast.

When Alfred learned of this, with the exception of a

83

small force which continued eastwards, he changed direction and marched with his army west towards Exeter. Arriving at London he was joined by citizens and reinforcements from the west, and continued east to Benfleet. Haesten had already arrived at Benfleet with his army which had been at Milton, and was joined there by the large army which had been at Appledore. Although most of the army was within the fortress which Haesten had built at Benfleet, when the English army arrived, Haesten himself was absent on a raid. The English army stormed and captured the fortress, bringing all of the goods and the women and children to London, destroying some of the ships and keeping others.

Among the captives were Haesten's wife and two sons which Alfred gave back to Haesten because one was his godson and the other the godson of ealdorman Æthelred, so Alfred must have previously had a treaty with Haesten at a time of which we know nothing about, before he attacked Benfleet. As with Guthrum, Alfred had dipped deep into his coffers in exchange for oaths and hostages, but Haesten had immediately broken his oaths, seizing Benfleet and ravaging the province of Æthelred, his son's godfather.

Tolerant of these broken treaties, or more likely unable to do otherwise, Alfred handed back the Danish king's wife and sons; and this time we hear no more of Haesten until he was killed on the Continent in 931.

When Alfred appeared at Exeter the Danes retreated to their ships. While Alfred was occupied here, others ravaged the country near Chichester and then the other two Danish armies assembled at Shoebury in Essex and went together up the Thames, reinforced by a number of Northumbrians and East Anglians. Travelling west as far as the Severn, they then ascended it. By this time a great part of the available English forces from west to east of the country, and including some Welsh, had assembled led by the Mercian ealdorman Æthelred, and overtook the Danish marauders at Buttington, laying siege to them. While this was taking place, Alfred was occupied in naval combats in Devon.

The siege of Buttington was resisted by the Danes for several weeks until many of them had died of starvation and the greater number of their horses had been eaten. The survivors finally burst out and a number escaped. Undeterred by this experience, when the survivors got back to Essex, they collected together a large army of Northumbrians and East Anglians. Leaving their women and ships in a safe place, they then made their way back west again and occupied a deserted fort at Chester.

Arriving too late to stop the Danes entering the fort, the English army seized the cattle which were outside and burnt the harvest, then besieging the fort for two days before apparently withdrawing. Perhaps, like Edward's division, their time was up and they simply went home content to take the cattle. Or they may have been alerted to the fact that the Danish pirate Sigeferth had left Northumbria and twice ravaged the coast and perhaps they went to prevent further attacks. Unable to survive at Chester, at the beginning of the next year (894) the Danish army moved into Wales and, pillaging as it went, then moved back eastwards across Northumbria into East Anglia, reaching the island of Mersea off the Essex coast.

But still the Danes had not had enough. Just before winter they sailed once more up the Thames and the River Lea, making a fortress on the Lea 20 miles above London. The following summer a local army marched on the fortress but was defeated, so in the autumn Alfred camped in the vicinity to enable the people to reap their harvest. He then blockaded the river at a narrow point so that the Danes would not be able to return with their boats. Seeing this the

Danes abandoned the boats and the rampaging horde travelled overland west to Bridgnorth on the Severn, where the Danes built another fortress and spent the winter.

The following summer (896) they divided, one force going to East Anglia and one to Northumbria, while a third part decided to try its hand in France. The Chronicle records that they had not afflicted the English people very greatly, a three-year plague of rinderpest or anthrax had a much more devastating effect upon both cattle and men (5). This suggests that the numbers of the Danish marauders were perhaps not so great as was generally made out.

Along the south coasts the Danes continued to harass Wessex so Alfred had a number of ships built to his own design, almost twice as long as the Danish ones, swifter and steadier, with more oars. When six pirate ships came to the Isle of Wight, Alfred then sent nine of his new vessels after them. Two of the Danish ships were captured and the occupants killed, while one ship escaped with only five men left alive. Unfortunately for the Anglo-Saxons, in their excitement they grounded their new ships, three of them on the side of the channel where the other three Danish ones had landed. The Danes now attacked these three ships killing 62 men as those of the other grounded ships watched helplessly, unable to come to their comrades' aid. This was not without an alleged loss of twice that number of men on the Danish side. When the tide turned, the Danish ships, being smaller and lighter, got off first. But so damaged were they that only one made it back to East Anglia, two being cast up on the Sussex shore. The occupants were rounded up and brought to Winchester, where Alfred ordered them all to be hung.

This at least spelt the end of piracy for the last three years of Alfred's reign.

Notes

1. Oak mildew is believed to have been imported from America at the beginning of this century.

2. Smyth (1995) dismisses it as invention.

3. The Anglo-Saxon Chronicle as we know it, is not one work but a group of texts differing from one another in date and place of origin, gathered together into a single narrative. All stem from an original compiled at some point in the later ninth century, probably in 896-7 at Winchester, continued and re-edited into the twelfth. Smyth (1995), in his closely argued 600-page blockbuster, deduces that Alfred instigated the Chronicle and had it edited to favour himself, its object being to follow his personal struggle with the Danes. It is Alfred's own personal policies and decisions that we are invited to study and admire, through playing down successive West Saxon defeats and diminishing the achievements of his older brothers by "a devious economy with the truth". Sturdy (1995) puts a quite different interpretation on the Chronicle's writing. It is to him "an austere, elegant and dignified piece of writing" with deliberate censorship "to clarify and enhance the drama."

4. Knott, P. 1990.

5. Rinderpest does not affect humans but the people were dependant upon cattle which were killed by it both for food and ploughing. It had ravaged the continent since 810 when it was spread by Charlemagne's army, and had probably been brought into England by the Danish invaders from

France when they landed in Kent in 892.

Chapter 4

Dispelling the Magic

Alfred the Myth

we possessed only the name of Christians,
and very few possessed the virtues.

Alfred. c890.

Great but not Perfect

I do not wish to be castigated as one of those responsible,
in Lappenberg's words, for "that conceited criticism, which,
hand in hand with desires subversive of all political institutions, threatens to annihilate both the learning and the
solid weal of Europe, and in its narrow ignorance efface the
memory of the greatest benefactor of this portion of the
globe". Faced with such disapprobation even the most ob-
jective of historians have quailed at the thought of the
merest hint of Alfred being anything other than the myth of
centuries purports him to be. Who would dare stand up to
the strictures of the Oxford don who at the beginning of the
century wrote: "It is pitiable that modern writers should
lend even half an ear to these wretched tales, which be-
smirch the fair fame of our hero king..." So there were
doubters, even before a recent "redbrick" university
Professor of Mediaeval History had the temerity to de-
nounce the thousand-year-old myth. But one can be great
without being perfect, whether it be King Alfred or Sir
Winston Churchill.

I would not concur with one of our modern historians

when he wrote of "this modest, gentle, scholarly man". Scholarly there is no question of otherwise, but I cannot imagine that a gentle man would have pursued the fierce Vikings over the Downs lopping off their heads, and succeed in welding together a barbarous and lawless nation into one in which none dared to break the law. And modest? Hardly, when we consider that he had the Anglo-Saxon Chronicle drawn up to suit his propaganda needs, glorifying his image and portraying him as the saviour-king, when in fact it was his inability to conquer the Danes which had led to the impoverished state of his nation in the first place.

The proud statue of Alfred overlooking Wantage market-place, his hand casually resting upon a giant axe; or that in Winchester where he holds aloft a mighty sword like the great Mimung forged by the father of Wayland; are probably closer to depicting Alfred's real character in his early years than the sculptors intended.

A late biographer, our old friend Thomas Hughes, attributed to Alfred: "Patience, humility, and utter forgetfulness of self, the true royal qualities, shine out through every word and act of his life wherever we can get at them." Hughes thought that for Alfred to have ever alienated his people by arrogance, impatience or superciliousness, was beyond anyone's belief: "So much then for the monkish tradition of Alfred's arrogant youth and its results", he wrote. But in his book "The Scouring of the White Horse" he makes his mysterious antiquary write that Alfred's rule was an unjust one in the early years of his reign. He was clearly taking this from "Asser", who wrote in his biography: "We may believe that this misfortune [a painful affliction] was brought upon the aforesaid king, because in the beginning of his reign, when he was a youth, and influenced by youthful feelings, he would not listen to the petitions which his subjects made to him for help in their necessities; but he drove them from him and paid no heed to their requests. This particular gave much pain to the holy man, St. Neot, who was his kinsman; and often foretold to him in the spirit of prophecy that he would suffer great adversity on this account; but Alfred neither attended to the reproof of the man of God, nor listened to his true prophecy - wherefore seeing that a man's sins must be corrected either in this world or the next, the true and righteous Judge willed that his sin should not go unpunished in this world, to the end that He might spare him in the world to come. From this cause, therefore, Alfred often fell into such great misery, that sometimes none of his subjects knew where he was, or what had become of him."

The allegations of tyranny and callousness in the early days of his reign were dismissed by the Oxford don Charles Plummer, as the "yet more silly story".

The only ancient chronicle which had the presumption to criticise Alfred, and that more than five hundred years after his death, has, in effect, been suppressed. Whereas others have been printed in various editions since the nineteenth century, and continue to be so for the benefit of scholars to this day, the last and only printed edition of John of Brompton's 1430 chronicle came out in 1652.

In the words of the German biographer Pauli, a truly wearisome task lies before author and reader when they attempt to investigate Alfred's life, for from the period of his accession throughout a great part of his reign it consists of an unbroken series of battles with the northern enemy. As far as knowledge of it goes, the reign of Alfred has been called a dark period of our history and almost all of our "knowledge" of it has derived from what was believed to be a contemporary biography of Alfred, nevertheless described as the strangest book in our mediaeval library.

91

Allegedly the biographer was an Anglo-Saxon-speaking Welsh monk brought up and ordained in the monastery of St. David, by name Asser Menevensis, who died in 910. It has been convincingly argued by Smyth (2) that this monk did not write the Life of Alfred. It was written a hundred years after Alfred's death, probably by a monk at Ramsey named Byrthferth. Most of it is copied from the Chronicle, which, togther with some other contemporary documents, tell us all that we know of Alfred. Historians now even regard the early part of the Chronicle as no more than a eulogy designed to glorify the West Saxon kings and their acts, rather than historical accounts of events, and it has been questioned whether before the fifth century contains any useful information whatsoever.

Alfred was 23 when the crown of greatness was thrust upon him, yet this was quite old as kings went in those days. Eadmund I was 18 years old when he became king in 940 and Eadgar, elected king of the Mercians in the stead of Eadwig in 959 was only 14. Eadward II (the Martyr) was 13 when he was made king in 975 and Ethelred, known as "the unready", only 10! Ethelred died in 1016 having reigned for 48 years. A boy's accountability, his capability of bearing arms, and of the management of his property, began according to earlier laws in his tenth year. Later, under the laws of Æthelstan (924-939), this was delayed until the twelfth year.

Alfred probably grew in esteem in the minds of people as under the harshness of the Norman kings the oppressed subjects longed for a happier past, and perhaps the monks painted word pictures of what kings ought to behave like for it would have meant torture and death to anyone who openly criticised the behaviour of a Norman king. By using Alfred as a model this criticism could be achieved indirectly. Thus at the beginning of the twelfth century the chronicler Florence of Worcester eulogised Alfred as that "famous, warlike, victorious king; the zealous protector of widows, scholars, orphans and the poor; skilled in the Saxon poets; affable and liberal to all; endowed with prudence, fortitude, justice and temperance; most patient under the infirmity which he daily suffered; a most stern inquisitor in executing justice; vigilant and devoted in the service of God." These virtues were manifestly not possessed by William II, and Florence's words could be seen as a covert diatribe against the reigning sovereign.

Little wonder that at the beginning of the thirteenth century an unknown poet extolled Alfred's virtues by calling him "Englene [England's] darling". His title "the Great" was somewhat belatedly bestowed upon his memory in the sixteenth century, unlike three other contintental kings of German race who were named likewise within some fifty years of their deaths: Theodoric, Charlemagne and Otto I. Also unlike these continental heroes, Alfred's name lapsed into the myth which still obscures it today. Byrthferth's aim in faking his Life of King Alfred was not to eulogise Alfred *per se*, but formed part of a great eleventh-century literary drive to further the aims of the ecclesiastical reformers in the aftermath of the Danish onslaught, seeking to provide an inspiration to the disciples of Monastic Reform. It was not the only such bogus production, but it was the one which was to catch the imagination of countless generations. To look at Alfred's life we have to ignore it completely as a factual source.

Skeletons in the Cupboard

Alfred was born in 847 or 848 and not in 849 as "Asser"

stated, but there is no record of his birth in the Chronicle. He was the youngest and last child of Osburh, wife of king Æthelwulf, and a woman whom Pauli fancifully described as "the ideal of a German mother. All her energies were devoted to her household..."

We have been led to believe by the Chronicle that in the year 853, at the tender age of five or six, Alfred was sent to Rome to receive the blessing of the Pope, and perhaps because of what he had heard from his young son of the splendours of Rome, two years later Æthelwulf himself set out for there allegedly taking Alfred with him on a second visit, although only Æthelwulf is mentioned in the Chronicle as undertaking this latter visit. Smyth (2) doubts whether Alfred ever went to Rome at all and considers that it was a contemporary fabrication inserted into the Chronicle to give Alfred prestige. Certainly two visits he considers to be taxing the imagination too far. That Æthelwulf went in 855 is established from other sources, but because there is no mention of the young Alfred with him, as he was of no consequence at the time this does not mean that he was not present. Both Caedwalla and Ine had made pilgrimages to Rome, dying and being buried there, and to show how much more powerful he was than they, Æthelwulf bore lavish gifts to Pope Benedict.

Returning, perhaps with Alfred, a year later, on reaching France Æthelwulf took a new wife. The 13-year old princess Judith, daughter of Charles the Bald, king of the West Franks. The possibility has been suggested that he had tired of Osburh because she is no longer referred to. But the king surely would not have flouted his Christian beliefs in so flagrant a manner immediately after leaving Rome, so the assumption is that she died.

Judith's youthful 13 years was probably the common age for girls to marry at that time. Indeed perhaps she was

94

already a little old for it! Æthelwulf was 60 at the time that he married Judith, betrothed in July he married her on October 1st at Verberie and she was crowned queen by his side.

That Æthelwulf's wife should be crowned queen was apparently a new departure from custom perhaps in deference to Christian ethics, for West Saxons had formerly granted no recognition to the royal spouse. "Asser" invented the story that this departure had been instituted because of the wanton behaviour of Eadburh, wife of Beorhtric, the previous king. His story was that due to the king's indulgence towards her this forceful woman had acquired an absolute dominion in all the internal concerns of the kingdom. Any whom she was opposed to she found the means to destroy either by false accusations or by poison. It was so with a young ealdorman named Worr who was a favourite of Beorhtric. In attempting to dispose of him she poisoned a drink which the king also took, perishing with his friend.

The wicked queen was obliged to flee taking her treasures with her and she made her way to the Continent to the court of Charlemagne. After being presented with gifts by her, the king jokingly inquired whether she would have him or his son. Whereupon she answered that she would have the son because he was younger. Charles, laughing, replied that if she had chosen him he would have given her his son, but now she should have neither. Instead he bestowed upon her a considerable monastery. This did not cause her to mend her ways, she was not long as abbess before she was convicted of licentious behaviour with a number of men and expelled from the convent by the king's orders. Left to wander, she died a beggar in the city of Pavia in 802.

Unfortunately the whole of this quaint story is

95

considered to be an invention designed to denigrate the memory of Offa and his hostile Mercians, making use of the popular theme of transformation which we encountered in the story of Alfred and the burning of the cakes. Here it is a queen who is transformed to menial status in a reversal of the Cinderella-role.

Upon Æthelwulf's death two years after his marriage, Æthelbald, Alfred's older brother, then married his father's young widow, according to "Asser" "contrary to God's prohibition and the dignity of a Christian, contrary also to the custom of all the Pagans". Some doubt has been cast on this marriage as possibly deriving from a confusion of Æthelbald with Eadbald, son of Æthelbert of Kent, recorded by Bede as having had an incestuous marriage with his step-mother. Although this suggestion is seemingly incorrect, the censure is apparently a late tenth or early eleventh century view and such a marriage was not contrary to pagan custom at the time. Indeed, the concern of the pope and others expressed later to Alfred about incest in England as an undesirable pagan hangover, suggests the marriage probably did take place. Fortunately Æthelbald's was a short reign, lasting for only two-and-a-half years.

After Æthelbald's death Judith, now 18, returned to her father's court, but then in defiance of her father eloped with a Flemish noble, Baldwin, to be married by the pope in Rome. Charlemagne then made Baldwin Count of Flanders.

Alfred has been described by some modern commentators as of exceptional religious devotion (3), yet he was quite prepared to overlook his stepmother's improprieties, and after he had ruled for six years, Pope John VIII had occasion to admonish him, exhorting him to respect the Archbishop of Canterbury and the rights and privileges of the Church, and to behave like his more godly predecessors if he wished to receive eternal salvation. He had also written to Æthelred, Archbishop of Canterbury: "We admonish you to set yourself as a wall for the house of God not only against the king, but also against all who are minded to act perversely." The pope was also concerned, in a letter to the archbishop's successor, Plegmund, about the laxity of the marriage vows in England, pointing out that no couple could separate except in the case of adultery, and then it was forbidden to remarry as long as both remained alive. Marriage was a contract for life. The pope also had to point out that relatives could not marry.

Nevertheless, some fifteen years or more after this admonition, Alfred gave his daughter Ælfthryth in marriage to Baldwin II count of Flanders, son of his stepmother by her second marriage, and thus Alfred's stepbrother; although not a blood relative. Matilda, the daughter of this union, was to become the wife of William the Conqueror.

Thirteen years later things still seem not to have changed much concerning what the archbishop of Reims termed the "incestuous heats of lasciviousness". About the year 890 the Archbishop wrote to Alfred congratulating him in appointing Plegmund as bishop of Canterbury, Alfred being concerned to eradicate the "perverse opinion of pagan errors" still surviving that allowed bishops and priests to have women living with them; intercourse between relatives; intercourse with nuns; and married men to have concubines. It seems that Alfred had not been as vigorous in suppressing these habits as he had been with some of his other endeavours, and was using the "sword of the word" in an attempt to change beliefs rather than make laws to enforce change. He tended to be liberal as far as sexual matters were concerned and his piety did not extend to a rigid imposition of the Bible's teachings on this subject. It has been argued that his priority was simply to revive the

97

standards of religious life and he could not go much further than that, but nevertheless, condemnation by word or deed for what was considered immoral by the Church was not forthcoming (4).

Alfred the Bookworm

We have to dismiss yet other inventions of Alfred's life by "Asser"; both his portrayal as a sickly youth, and that in the middle of his marriage ceremony he was suddenly seized by a malady. Said perhaps to be the return of a painful disease from which he had suffered much in his earliest youth it was described as a kind of fit like an epilepsy, but probably in reference to the earlier affliction "Asser" referred to it as the ficus or haemorrhoids.

We are told that Alfred's schooling was ignored by his parents and next that he was a precocious reader. Then it is claimed that he was illiterate until he was 39. Another invention was the famous story of Alfred's eagerness to read: "One day, his mother showed him and his brothers a beautiful volume, filled with Saxon poetry, and said, "The one among you children who can first say this book by heart, shall have it." Alfred came forward and eagerly asked his mother, "Wilt thou really give it to the one who learns it the quickest and repeats it to thee?" Osburh smiled for joy, and said, "Yes to him will I give it." So Alfred went off with his teacher and learnt the coveted volume by heart.

Had the story been true, Alfred's reply to his mother probably would have sounded just like you would have heard it from a Berkshire lad less than fifty years ago: "Ull ee gie un to oi, if oi be the fust to larn un?"

Alfred probably was well educated in his early youth

98

otherwise he is unlikely to have been able to study and translate the difficult Latin texts that he was to in later life. The enthusiasm for study which he later displayed make his visits to Rome all the more probable, for such visits at a highly impressionable age would have influenced him for the rest of his life, forming the driving force behind his desire to re-establish a culture in England. But not long after his alleged second return from Rome Alfred would have been called to the battlefield. By the time that he was crowned, in the 'midst of warfare,' he had already seen several years' service and his reign was to give him little respite from fighting.

Alfred's Reign

When we forget the posthumous panegyric of the pseudo-Asser and learn what we can of Alfred's reign from the greatly biased Chronicle, a very different Alfred emerges. Reading between the lines we can detect a tough, wily and scheming king, always promoting his own image and once peace had come after the baptism of Guthrum, it appears that he may have held the reins of government more tightly than before, attempting to despotically weld a tightly-run state from the loose political relations. It has been alleged that he attempted to narrow the ancient liberties of the people. The hereditary sovereignty of the earls over their particular districts began to disappear, the earls becoming simply officers of the court, and the church elders no longer participated in actual affairs of state outside of their offices. Alfred was establishing the royal prerogative. Even the adulatory Pauli was forced to concede: "We cannot deny the tendency towards despotism which he introduced into the government, this is evinced in various instances."

Nevertheless he had the *witan*, "wise men", to contend with. Whereas it has been argued that this was little more than a bunch of cronies who paid obeisance to the king, Smyth contends that it was a powerful upper-class body of the king's advisers with the collective power to depose a king as well as elect one. Election may have been obtained by buying its support, but no contender could come to power or rule without that support either in Alfred's reign or after it. But it was not the first example of democracy which the Victorians wished to believe of it, but composed of thegns or nobles, and bishops. The common people had no part in it. Whereas inheritance might have decided who the candidates for succession to the crown might be, it was the witan which appeared to exercise the decisive role. But it is not known how one became a member of the *witan*.

No Law-Maker

The power and lawlessness of the nobles may have greatly increased during the years of war and devastation, and through their influence the courts of justice had been virtually suppressed. Among the justices, in consequence of their ignorance both of law and of basic knowledge, the greatest discord prevailed and most of the cases had to be brought before the king's court for final arbitration. But Alfred also constantly reviewed the judgements of cases decided in the inferior courts, and often found that he had to instruct the judges. Allegedly there were 44 cases of execution of judges for awarding unjust or inconsiderate sentences, information which only comes down to us from a fourteenth century work "Miroir des Justices" by Andrew Horne. Some consider this to be a disguised attack upon Edward II and nothing to do with Alfred.

Alfred drew up a Domboc or Book of Laws, containing 48 "dooms", as they were called; introducing them with a discussion of the Old and New Testaments, quoting the Ten Commandments and extracts from Exodus, to underline the sacred nature of kingship and its power to ordain, as well as being a public display of this royal power. The obligation of an oath apparently had no sanction attached to it by West Saxon law until Alfred enforced it in his code. Apparently copying Charlemagne this included a general oath of loyalty to the king, Alfred perhaps having in mind the lack of support which he encountered after his defeat at Chippenham. In connection with breaking an oath the first mention is made of imprisonment, where 40 nights is specified.

In his compilation of laws Alfred introduced some changes, but as he himself informs us, he did not venture to insert many enactments of his own as he doubted whether they would be approved by his successors. Written laws usually represented the codification of established custom, not the invention of new restraints.

So the title of lawgiver is erroneous. He created few new laws, his aim was simply to restore, renovate and improve; correcting and revising the old laws into a comprehensive system to meet changing times and produce the first restatement for almost a century. Amongst particular tribes and following conversion to Christianity, some laws had already been committed to writing. The perfection of a written language in the West Saxon dialect, earlier than on the Continent, has been seen as tending to limit the power of the clergy, albeit unintentionally, in much greater degree

101

than was possible on the Continent, for people did not have to rely any longer solely upon what the clergy and Rome, told them. Kent, Wessex, and Mercia, each had its own laws. Alfred could resort to the Kentish laws of Æthelbert (c602), the first Christian king, with their subsequent additions; the West Saxon laws of Ine (drawn up between 688-694), and the Mercian laws of Offa. Those of Ine, as well as incorporating in part, he also included in their entirety as an appendix. Alfred amended where necessary to replace paganism with Christianity, and the establishment of the royal authority. To the latter end he introduced a law in which conspiracy against the king's life, even indirectly, was punishable with death and loss of property.

In his laws the king's *wergild* was made higher than an archbishop's, reversing the older law. The fine for breaking the king's bail was five pounds' weight of coin, for breaking an archbishop's three pounds. For breaking into the king's house, 120 shillings fine; for an archbishop's house 90. Nonetheless, all were to be judged equally. Alfred was the first to enunciate that there should not be one law for the rich and another for the poor. Although his scale of *wergild* could be seen as contradicting this, we have the same system in English law today whereby offenders pay a fine according to their means. The judgement of course, is not the penalty. But Alfred's penalties could be harsh. For public slander the offender's tongue was to be cut out.

No Shire-Maker

It is a myth that Alfred was the first to divide the country into shires, hundreds and tithings. These divisions, perhaps based upon tribal divisions dating from the Bronze Age, inherited by the Iron Age, and adapted by the Romans, were in turn probably inherited in the first Anglo-Saxon settlement which took them over in the fifth century (5). But it is only in the first half of the ninth century that they may have become recognised as shires, and not until Alfred's time were they committed to writing in a general defence survey of Wessex known as the Burghal Hidage, in which the burhs and their hides were set out. Apparently copying Charles the Bald, Alfred drew up a plan for the defence of each fortified position or burh, by assessing the number of hides of land associated with it, each hide being obliged to contribute one man. Listing only thirty places this plan is far from being a Domesday Survey but may have formed its basis. The surviving document is a revision dating from 914-919.

It was much later that the shires were subdivided into hundreds and then tythings, each with its own court, the hundred-court and the courts-leet; and not until the time of Cnut that every man in the country was obliged by law to belong to a tything, or if he lived in a town to a guild, and anyone not belonging to either was apparently an outlaw.

Whatever reforms Alfred effected in the administration of justice and the organisation of the country, these were almost all adaptations or developments of what he found when he acceded to the throne. Many of the institutions had long been common property to all the Germanic nations, but were particularly developed among the Anglo-Saxons.

The system credited to Alfred of changing from fighting roaming pitched battles to setting up a chain of fortified positions or burhs may have been inspired by Frankish practice, but he would have been familiar with the great ancient Downland forts such as Uffington and Segsbury Castles. They were given Anglo-Saxon names and they may have been used in connection with the battle of

Ashdown. But it was Charles the Bald who first measured out the length of fortifications (on the Seine) and assigned responsibility for so many men per length, and the obligation of landowners to supply defenders according to the amount of land they possessed. Charles's defensive bridge-building, guarding of rivers on both banks and the building of forts on river banks with fortified bridges, all reappear in the Chronicle under Alfred's name (2).

The Oft-Defeated King

As to Alfred's military capabilities, although they have been much lauded he never seems to have won a battle, despite several times fighting the Danes to a stalemate and then entering into a treaty with them. Ashdown was perhaps not so much his victory as the king's. Unlike "Asser's" fictional account in which Alfred made a "boar-like charge", the only dissident chronicle, that of John of Brompton, states that Alfred engaged too hastily and was "near upon retreating", when the king came up with fresh forces and together they put the Danes to flight. Had it not been for the king, Alfred would have been overcome.

And what are we to make of one allegedly so pious and devout yet so impatient of prayer before battle? Instead of observing Mass with the king he allegedly rushed out to attack the enemy by himself. Deeds, not words, seems to have been his motto. Impatience, not humility, his character.

He could not have been held in great esteem in his early kingly career, for in the year 878 he was deserted by the majority of his nobles and people after the humiliating

104

defeat at the battle of Chippenham, obliging him to flee to Athelney.

Even the military strategy with which he was credited, of having half of the available fighting men in the field at any one time while the other half rested, was not an original idea. He was simply implementing what his ancestors the Suebi, the most warlike of all the German tribes, had done almost a thousand years before. He probably got the idea from reading Julius Caesar's *De Bello Gallico*, Caesar's own account of his wars in Gaul and Britain. In view of the Roman inheritance in Britain, this surely must have been one of Alfred's most carefully studied books. He would almost certainly have read it in connection with the translation of the fifth century world history of Paulus Orosius "Seven Books of Histories against the Pagans" which he had had prepared by an unknown West Saxon.

Alfred's intention in having Orosius's Histories translated into Anglo-Saxon was much more than that of simply providing a history book in the native tongue, it was to combat the growing pagan opposition to Christianity. As with the fall of the Roman Empire, the pagans claimed that the troubles of the time were due to the introduction of the Christian faith, probably resulting from a lack of sacrifices to appease the gods. Pope Gregory I had stated that whereas the people were accustomed to sacrifice many oxen in honour of demons, they should rather eat the animals in praise of God. Orosius dwelt on the catastrophes befalling mankind before the coming of Christianity, thereby arguing against the view that the evils and perils of the Roman Empire were a sequel of its conversion to Christianity.

When it came to shipbuilding and his idea of building bigger ships than those of the Danes, we must remember that the Danes' intention was to operate rather like marine commandos. Their ships were not for fighting sea battles but more for use as landing craft. They needed small, shallow-draught boats in order to penetrate inland via the rivers. A river such as the Ock, which although in Anglo-Saxon times was undoubtedly much more than the shallow brook it is today, was still not a major waterway like the Thames. As we saw, Alfred's ships (almost twice as long as the normal vessels), ran aground at the first coastal engagement, and could not be got off again as quickly as the shorter and shallower Danish boats. In principle they undoubtedly would be superior for challenging the Danish boats at sea, although Plummer asked why should it be necessary to take them on at sea at all? On the other hand, it has been argued, it was important to prevent them from landing and enlisting the support of their countrymen already settled in England. Thus the most effective strategy was to destroy their ships before landing, together with their supplies and their means of escape.

Again Alfred's inspiration probably came from Caesar's *De Bello Gallico*, with its description of the superior ships of the Veneti which were bigger and heavier and with flat bottoms: "Their timbers were all oak, to withstand the roughest violence. The cross-timbers were a foot thick and riveted with iron bolts as thick as a man's thumb. Iron chains, not ropes, held the anchors...."

Other Errors

One early biographer suggested that Alfred was the first to build in stone, but of course the Romans had built in stone and fired clay long before, using clay tiles for roofing. It was the ravages, first of the Anglo-Saxons themselves and then of the Danes, which laid waste these buildings and rendered solid habitations a liability as we have seen. Alfred only created the conditions towards the end of his reign which made a return to more permanent building possible.

As to his work as an author he could not possibly have translated, paraphrased and adapted all the books which were once attributed to him. It is no doubt to his monks and bishops that we owe these works, albeit undertaken at Alfred's instigation and probably overseen by him. Nevertheless what he did translate himself, such as Boethius's "On the Consolation of Philosophy", show that he had a very good grasp of Latin and indeed of learning, justly deserving of the title of scholar-king.

Alfred led us to believe that at the beginning of the ninth century it was in Wessex and the country south of the Thames that the greatest ignorance prevailed in consequence of the Danish invasion, and any seeds of a higher civilisation and education were threatened with annihilation, but this was due to his own inability to contain the Danes. Alfred however turned this shortcoming on his part into pretending that it was a situation which he had inherited and which he then set out to remedy. In his Preface to his translation of the "Regula Pastoralis" of Gregory I, Alfred wrote that "So entirely has knowledge escaped from the English people, that there are few on this side of the Humber who can understand the divine service, or even explain a Latin epistle in English; and, I believe, not many on the other side of the Humber either. But they are so few, that indeed I cannot remember one south of the Thames, when I began to reign."

At the same time he recalled that when he was young he had seen, "ere all within them was laid waste and burnt up, how the churches throughout all the English race stood filled with treasures and books, also a great multitude of God's servants, though they knew very little use of those books, for that they could not understand anything of them." When he was eighteen the Danes had destroyed the library at York, famed the century before as one of the greatest libraries in western Europe.

If we were to take Alfred's comments on learning too literally we would have to write off not only the survival of Latin, but of Early English Christianity itself for much of the ninth century and the first half of the tenth. Alfred was trying to bolster his own achievements and also persuade the bishops to accept the need for education and his translation programme. (2) But his cultural programme was more modest than his many past biographers have asserted. Few in Alfred's day would have been able to read at the best of times, let alone understand, his translations; and they contributed little if anything to a basis for educational reform of the young. Apart from his translation of the Psalms, his specialized translation programme could have been of interest only to a small scholarly elite. Few outside of his immediate scholarly circle are likely to have read his translations of Boethius's Consolation or St. Augustine's Soliloquies, and fewer still of his bishops or thegns could have understood Alfred's philosophical interpretations of the works. Yet by their very obliquity these works would have served to enhance his personal position by endowing him with an almost magical command of wisdom and learning.

Alfred and the Church

"Asser", writing a hundred years later when conditions were much more prosperous, was not sure if the monasteries failed to attract novitiates because of the frequent and savage attacks by the Danes which disrupted normal life, or because of the people's enormous abundance of riches "of every kind". Suggestions which appear to contradict one another. "Asser" thought the latter explanation the more likely, the people looking with contempt on monastic life because of their riches. But after years of harrowing by the Danes hardly an abbey, mansion or cottage had escaped destruction and the Anglo-Saxons had to think more about defending themselves than defending the faith. "Asser's" assertion that no one directed a rule of life in a regular way was hardly surprising. Education was confined to the ecclesiastics and in the years of devastation and turmoil the number of older learned monks had disappeared and younger ones were not forthcoming. We may suppose that in a land where so much war had taken place young men were at a premium, both for other activities and as marriage partners. Few would wish to seek the celibate life of a monastery.

There were also other causes for decline. Prior to the death in 870 of Ceolnoth, Archbishop of Canterbury, there had in one year been such great mortality amongst his monks that only five were left for the work of the Cathedral, and he was obliged to bring in to assist the surviving monks some of the priests of the vills who derived from the ceorls and lacked the education of the monks.

Christianity had already exercised considerable influence over the intellectual culture of the nation. In Wessex the first episcopal see was at Dorcic, or Dorchester as we now know it, where St. Birinus first baptised Cynegils and his followers. From this see a bishopric at Winchester was afterwards detached, Dorchester retaining Hampshire and Surrey.

It is doubtful if Alfred made much attempt to revive monastic life and doubtful if he built a monastery at Athelney and a convent at Shaftesbury; nor endowed an abbey at Amesbury in Wiltshire which by Domesday had possessions at Kintbury, North Fawley and West Challow on the Berkshire Downs. He did not live long enough to see his plans for founding a new minster at Winchester carried out, if indeed he ever had such plans. He did however invite men of eminence from Mercia, such as Plegmund whom he raised to Archbishop of Canterbury in 899, and Wærferth, appointed to the see of Worcester. And he may have invited foreign scholars to England, among whom was Grimbald, provost of St. Omer's. It would have been natural for Alfred to send to Frankland for scholars as its schools were envied even by the Greeks at this time, and his father had employed a Frank named Felix as secretary.

Alfred presumably chose Winchester as his capital because he believed that his ancestors, the first West Saxon invaders, had originated there. Winchester already boasted a substantial stone seventh century church, a stone structure being a rarity for a Saxon church at this time. But the story of Alfred's embassy to Fulke, Archbishop of Rheims and to the abbot of St. Bertin's monastery, requesting the secondment of Grimbald, the emissaries conveying a gift of wolf-hounds for which Archbishop Fulke said he gave in return a spiritual watch-dog to guard the Christian flock; is yet another quaint story which must be consigned to folklore.

Alfred's alleged construction of a monastery at Athelney, placing an Old Saxon, John, at its head, and staffing it with youths from the Continent so that the people changed its name from Athelney to Alienissa, the house of aliens; is yet another story, dressed up with the tale of how two Frankish monks, a priest and a deacon, conspired against the Old Saxon abbot, paying two slaves to murder him in church when he was praying alone: "But he heard the sound made by the first movement of the murderers, and not being ignorant of the use of arms, he defended himself until others came to his assistance." Although severely wounded he escaped with his life.

Equally without factual basis is the story that Alfred founded the nunnery at Shaftesbury and having endowed it together with the convent at Winchester, placed his second daughter Æthelgivu in it as abbess. She was supposedly of infirm health, hardly a fitting person to control a nunnery dedicated to the rigour of Benedictine Rule. Athelney, Shaftesbury and the Winchester nunnery, were all founded after Alfred's death. His queen Ealhswith is credited with erecting and endowing the abbey of St. Mary in Winchester for nuns, where she might retreat after the death of her husband to end her days, but there is no evidence to suppose that Alfred assisted her, and it was completed after her death. Only after Alfred's death did Winchester develop into the mighty Abbey of Hyde.

Whatever Alfred may or may not have done, new life was infused into the Church. Alfred desired that the whole kingdom might advance in civilisation and morality. But he did not limit himself to the Church and stated that all the freeborn youth of his people "who are rich enough to be able to devote themselves to it should be sent to learn as long as they are not fit for any other occupation" until they could read English, others continuing and learning Latin. But this did not imply that he was setting up a system of schools, the people charged with the responsibility for this teaching were the bishops who were to organize it in their

111

cathedral schools. Such a school had already existed in Canterbury in the seventh century. Clearly Alfred was not interested in a popular educational system, but only in the elite. More like schools for civil service mandarins, for: "..those... who are to continue learning and be promoted to a higher rank". He did not, however, found the University of Oxford, a spurious claim introduced into an edition of "Asser" by the antiquarian William Camden in 1603. Camden attempted to imply that Oxford University was in existence before Alfred's time and therefore much earlier than Cambridge, leading a distinguished nineteenth century Oxford history don to comment drily that the earliest form of inter-university sports seems to have been a competition in lying.

One of the first effects of Alfred's revival of the church was to attract the notice of Pope Marinus who in 882 or 883 sent an embassy to Alfred with presents, including "a part of the rood on which Christ suffered". Alfred sent presents in return in 883 with two of his nobles, Sigehelm and Æthelstan. Although an apparent annual exchange of courtesies and an annual present to the Pope followed, the relations between the Pope and the English Church do not appear to have become more intimate. In some respects Alfred asserted his superiority over the national church and over its highest ministers, more so than his predecessors. The way in which he addressed and employed his bishops, taking them about with him and giving them translations and other work to do, shows that he considered them to be his officers, and that they acknowledged his authority. In the last years of his reign he left all the sees of Wessex vacant and only under the care of the Archbishop of Canterbury. The pope did not even remonstrate with him, but after his death threatened his successor with excommunication if the sees were not filled up.

Alfred shows himself to have been more interested in culture and learning than religion itself and does not emerge as a very devout king. But as with his predecessors, Christianity had a lot to offer a king with its concepts of the divine nature of the constituted authority, giving the king a very exalted role. Supported by his bishop the king had access to sources of power and prestige which the pagan kings did not, thus almost everywhere kings were the first converts. With the aid of Boethius's Consolation Alfred was developing in his own mind a new model of kingship, an essentially Christian model of a king who did not rely on terror or conquest for the enforcement of his authority. Perhaps indeed he did not develop this view from reading Boethius alone, but had learnt it from the compromises he had had to make with the Danes and the many occasions on which he had had to eat humble pie in order to appease them. Since he could not set himself up as a mighty warrior he promoted the idea that the acquisition of wisdom led to power. In the new order men would be ruled by a philosopher-king who had come reluctantly to power in order to prevent the tyranny of the wicked (2). Boethius had affirmed a reluctance to hold high office which gave Alfred the idea to present himself as the reluctant ruler (7).

Scarcely anything is known of the last four years of his life. Alfred died on the 26th October 899 aged 51 or 52 years, having reigned for 29 years 6 months, but no particulars are recorded of the place where he died nor of how he died. Surprising omissions if he had been held in great esteem. In spite of his religious convictions, Alfred did not abdicate to find salvation in a monastery in his later years as some of his predecessors had, but then Alfred died younger than those who had become monks and who perhaps had felt that they had become too old to hold on to power. His death was probably rather sudden and the

113

apparent meanness with which he treated his nephews in his will showed him at the ultimate hour in a less than favourable light.

Alfred was first buried in the church of St. Swithun at Winchester because the monastery was not yet built. When it was finally dedicated in 903, his son and successor, Edward, had Alfred's body exhumed and buried in the Abbey because the canons allegedly asserted that the royal spirit, resuming its carcase, wandered nightly through the buildings.

Alfred showed great ability in government and administration compared with his predecessors, but times were changing and England was becoming more and more a unified state, no longer a chequer-board of war lords defending each his own and seizing advantage over the weaker whenever they could.

By the time that he was able to sit down and write after a lifetime of sporadic warfare, he professed great humility and modesty, but perhaps it was all part of the image of himself which he wished to promote based on the writings of Boethius, for it contrasts strongly with his view of himself as divinely appointed and his statement that "all of them [men arriving at the court of their king] live through the one lord's favour". "You know that covetousness and greed for wordly dominion never pleased me over much, and that I did not all too greatly desire this earthly rule..", he wrote. But if anyone promoted the concept of the divine rule of kings, it was Alfred.

If his father did send him to Rome at the impressionable age of five or six, then this would explain what made him the great seeker after learning that he was, and imbued him with a desire not to let the country become a barbaric enclave of the pagan Danes. He wanted his country to reflect the civilized splendour of Rome with its great buildings, not the lowly barbarism of the thatched long hall. Other kings went to Rome too late in life for the experience to motivate them in the same way that it would a young mind.

He showed a deep sense of the responsibility of kingship when he wrote, "..I desired tools and material for the work that I was charged to perform, namely that I might worthily and fittingly steer and rule the dominion that was entrusted to me."

"..I desired to live worthily as long as I lived, and to leave after my life, to the men who should come after, my memory in good works."

Above all, he sought to be remembered as a Christian king.

Pauli aptly summed it up: "So stands the image of Alfred, shining brightly in the book of world's history, never defaced by malice or ignorance, nor dimmed by his own errors. These he necessarily possessed, but they have been entirely forgotten in the blaze of his virtues, over which the lapse of centuries has cast no cloud....."

Two recent authorities on the life of Alfred (3), following in the adulation bestowed upon him by their predecessors, conclude that when judged in purely military and political terms, Alfred's achievement was impressive; when judged also in cultural terms, it was truly exceptional. But they also concede that when he died his achievements were far from secure, and it remained for those who came after to ensure that the promise of his reign was properly fulfilled by kings such as Æthelstan and Edgar. What Egbert began, Alfred developed, and his successors completed. His mistakes and failures as a military leader are seldom admitted in the Chronicle, and when they are organizational failure at local level or lack of loyalty to the king himself are hinted at as the causes for blame. Nevertheless, Alfred may have lost most of his battles, but in the end he

115

did not lose the war.

More Machiavellian than saintly in his early years, he has nevertheless been canonized by the Catholic church. Known as Saint Alfred the Great, his saint's day is October 26th (8).

Notes

1. Plummer, C. 1902.

2. Smyth, A.P. 1995.

3. Keynes, S. and Lapidge, M. 1983.

4. Some critics argue that Alfred could not be expected to conform to Victorian views of morality, but it is an anachronism to call the views of a ninth century pope "Victorian". The moral stance of the Pope was probably a reaction to the habits of the time and an attempt to create a more humane and more ordered society. Just as Victorian morality was a reaction to the harsh economics of the time brought about by the Industrial Revolution, and just as moral attitudes in Britain today are simply a reflection of the economics of the time brought about by the welfare state.

5. See Gelling, M. 1976, Pt. III, pp 800-812, for a discussion of this.

6. Alfred's prefatory letter to his translation of Pope Gregory's Pastoral Care.

7. Anicius Manlius Severinus Boethius (c480-524) was a

Roman scholar, philosopher, theologian and statesman. Holder of some of the highest offices of state he was accused of conspiring against the king Theodoric and imprisoned. While awaiting execution he wrote his greatest work, "The Consolation of Philosophy". Dealing with philosophy and theology it ignores the possibility of finding consolation in any Christian belief, but concludes that God rewards the good and punishes the wicked.

8. "The Book of Saints", 1989.

The Vale

Chapter 5

The View from the Vale

Was Alfred born here?

I pity people who weren't born in a vale. I don't
mean a flat country, but a vale: that is, a flat
country bounded by hills. The having your hill
always in view if you choose to turn towards him,
that's the essence of a vale. There he is for ever
in the distance, your friend and companion; you
never lose him as you do in hilly districts.

Thomas Hughes. 1857.

Introduction to the Cow Road

Instead of climbing upwards to the Downs as we did from
Uffington with Thomas Hughes, let us wend our way down
into the Vale from Wantage, following the road Thomas
Hardy did a hundred years ago when he walked from his
grandmother's Downland village of Fawley to Wantage
Road Station. Yet not stopping here, but carrying on
towards Christminster, or Oxford as we more properly
know it; through King's Grove and crossing the King's
Boundary, until we reach East Hanney. Here we come to
"Fiveways", sadly changed in aspect since its ancient inn
"The Plough" became a modern restaurant, but the two
chestnut trees on the green planted at the end of last century
still with their original iron circular seats around them; the
great village elm or "Cross-tree" now a sorry stump, victim

119

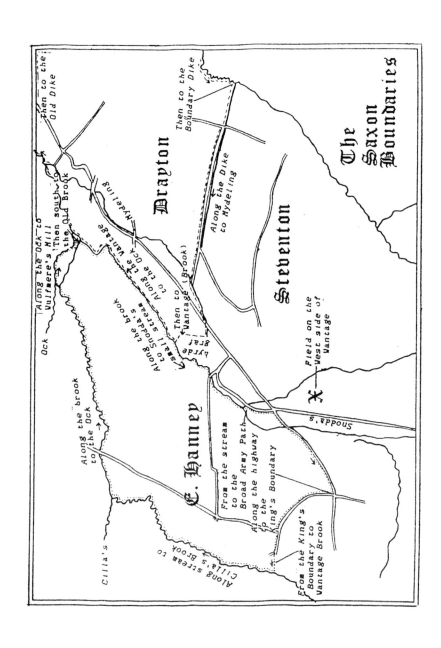

The Saxon Boundaries

to the Dutch elm disease .

Anglo-Saxons dubbed the place *hanena ieg* or "island of wild birds". No Roman or other early remains have been found here because it was probably a damp, unhealthy island, encircled by a swampy Letcombe Brook. The Anglo-Saxons may have first occupied Hanney and neighbouring islands, such as Goosey and Charney, because their reedy fastnesses provided places in which to hide from marauding Danes; just as Alfred was to hide in the Athelney marshes.

Up on the Downs we saw how the different peoples of history had left their indelible mark upon the landscape until the time of the ancestors of Alfred. Here, in the Vale beneath, there is little sign of any impressive monuments being raised. No Wessex pyramids elevate their rounded forms, nor sarsen cromlechs hide a mystic past. Nonetheless, these early peoples were leaving their mark. Cherbury Camp near Charney suggests that at one time the Bronze Age inhabitants perhaps did raise structures others of which have now disappeared under the plough.

On the whole they seem to have been less able or less ambitious here; perhaps defeated by the stiff, clay soil. If they had built barrows with it the barrows would surely have persisted. Instead we find, near Drayton for example, a small mound with but a single burial. Excavated in 1826, this Iron Age burial mound revealed the skeleton of a man, an urn, a bronze ring and some bones. Now cut through by the railway line to the south, an old Steventon field name, "beggars' patch" is probably a corruption of Old English *beorg*, indicating there was once a tumulus in the area.

The Roman period left the most evidence, but contrary to the casual impression of an uninteresting expanse of intensively cultivated fields, the area conceals beneath its surface numerous remains of an historic past from the

121

Stone Age to mediaeval times. Stone Age worked flints, Bronze Age, Iron Age, Romano-British and Anglo-Saxon pottery remains; have all been found within this area east of Fiveways.

Position yourself out in the large field to the south of the road to Steventon after the harvest has been gathered in and the cropped ground spreads before you as flat as can be. Look at the vast vista stretching into the distance to the Corallian moors and you can actually feel that you are standing on the bed of the once great Ice Age lake which covered this expanse. This is the land of which an Oxford agriculturist wrote in 1916:

"To stand on the hill immediately to the west of Drayton and look up the Vale at sunset is to obtain one of the most beautiful views in Berkshire or in any part of England. Almost due west, about eleven miles distant, Faringdon clump stands in the middle of the scene, and the foreground has the appearance of a rich valley with the woods of Steventon and the rising ground forming the boundary on the south."

In the north this area is bounded by the River Ock, the river up which the earliest West Saxon settlers made their way in the fifth century to reach the Romano-British settlement at Frilford. The river's name is a rare Bronze or Iron Age survival from *Eocca*, or salmon river. Nearly a thousand years later it was noted for its pike rather than any other fish, but the salmon was one of numerous animals regarded as sacred by the Celts and perhaps it was just a name rather than implying that salmon actually occurred there. In the 1940s I found it inhabited by a giant trout, too old and wise to be caught by my boyish endeavours, so huge that its dorsal fin stuck out above the shallow waters sending pulsating waves across the surface wherever it rested under the overhanging bank. For the Ock is now little more than a shallow brook which would no longer take an Anglo-Saxon boat, although, as the poet Drayton expressed it in 1613, it drains the White Horse Hill country to the Thames:

That White-horse, for the love she bare to her ally And honour'd sister Vale, the bounteous Aylsebury, Sent presents to the Tame by Ock her only Flood..

The Ock is joined in the west by Childrey or Cilla's brook, taking its name after Ceolswyth, or Cille for short, sister of Hha, the lady said to have founded a nunnery at Helnestoue or Helen-stow (St. Helen's Church, Abingdon) about 700, but for some reason moved it to the top of Wytham hill near Oxford until ejected from there by Offa eighty years later. How the brook came to be named after her is not known. It is joined in its turn by Letcombe Brook, or Leoda's valley brook, which flows through East Hanney bordering the west of our area. To the east lies the village of Drayton, a name thought to derive from the need to use a kind of sledge or *draeg* to get through the mud, hence *draeg tun*. And then south of this once important royal Anglo-Saxon vill lies Steventon, or Stifa's tun, even possibly "stump town". Then in the south the area stretches away to the Downs and the downland villages of West Hendred, Ardington and Lockinge.

Roughly from south to north through the centre flows Cow Common Brook, anciently known as Wantage Brook, marking the boundary between East Hanney and Steventon and Drayton since Anglo-Saxon times, and probably well before that. No more than a narrow stream today, as ancient field names indicate it was once big enough to have an eel fishery along its reaches, probably to supply the Black Monks of Steventon Priory. Diagonally across the area, following the line of an ancient Bronze Age road which was later to become the Anglo-Saxon's broad army-path or *bradan here-pæd*, is the derelict Wilts and Berks Canal, its overgrown willow-clad banks now the secret home of badgers and deer. Constructed in 1808, opened in 1810, dry by 1903, is its epitaph; the coal barge trade snatched away by the Great Western Railway which in 1840 cut across the south of the area from east to west with its roaring monsters.

The East Hanney fields were inclosed in 1803 and the lands bordering the brook lost their common ownership. But on the Steventon side common lands persisted until 1885 as agreement on inclosure could not be reached. When it finally came about a road was made to join that from East Hanney which had terminated at the brook.

Steventon fields still show many of the offset corners which indicated the boundary of a strip field, many marked by the planting of oak trees at inclosure, those few remaining now of fine stature. Some of these corners still remain in the Hanney fields, often now no more than a kink in an otherwise straight hedge, but there are no oaks to mark them on the Hanney side. The market for oak collapsed in 1850 so perhaps they planted elms instead, destroyed in the 1970s by Dutch elm disease.

John Rocque's "Topographical Map of Berkshire" shows the area treeless in 1761, and by the time of the inclosures the fields between Hanney and the parish boundary were already large. But old field names, now long forgotten, show that there were woods here in Anglo-Saxon times. To the north was Tippany Wood, a name probably deriving from Old English *Timper*, or a place in which to get wood for building; in the centre was *Hyrde graf*, the grove of the shepherds; while further south and on the east of Wantage Brook the name of Hayward's Walk indicates the former existence of a ride through an enclosed wood here, perhaps the deer preserve for Steventon Priory (Old English *(ge)hæg* and *wudu* = hayward). But this would have been much later, deer parks achieving importance in the thirteenth century. To the west, near Ardington Marsh, was a field called "In the barrow", probably corrupted from "in the *bearu*" or wood; joining with, or an outlier of, King's grove (or it could refer to *beorg* indicating a former tumulus in the area).

The Ancient Charters

Due to the various gifts of land disbursed by Anglo-Saxon kings, (Alfred gave away no land in this area, his will suggests that he owned only Wantage and Lambourn in Berkshire - 1) the boundaries of East Hanney were described in ancient charters which have come down to us, both in 956 and again in 968; and those of Drayton in 958 and 960. No charters survive to indicate if Steventon was given away.

That of East Hanney in 956 read: "First from the king's boundary to wantage [Letcombe] brook. Along the stream until it comes out to cilla's brook then along the brook until it comes out to the Ock. Then along the Ock until it comes to wulfmere's mill [near the site of present Marcham Mill]. Then south to the old brook. Along the brook until it comes to snodda's small stream. From the small stream to the broad army-path. Along the army-path until it comes once more to the king's boundary" (2).

For Drayton in 958 the description for our area read: "...then to the boundary ditch. Along the ditch to mydeling. Then to wantage [brook]. Along the wantage to the ock..."

125

The later version had instead of "Then to wantage", "up from mydeling to the north side of the grove of the herdsmen. Then straight to wantage."

These descriptions show that the boundaries of the present-day parishes were already established and their outlines and general topography were to remain virtually unchanged until the transport revolution of the nineteenth and twentieth centuries. Probably the limits had their origins in Iron Age boundaries adopted and modified by the Roman administration. Then the Anglo-Saxon chiefs or kings apportioned this land among themselves and granted estates to their nobles. While at first the land was owned by ceorls, free men and Anglo-Saxon royalty, the establishment of Abingdon Abbey in the seventh century led to the Abbey acquiring extensive estates as well as tithes in the area.

Much of this area in Anglo-Saxon times originally belonged to the kings. Thus in 728 King Ine allegedly granted Sutton to Abingdon Abbey but this does not seem to have been honoured, Sutton still being in the royal gift in 983 and until the reign of Henry II (1154). In 931 Æthelstan, ealdorman of East Anglia, granted an estate at Uffington to the church of St. Mary at Abingdon, but in 953 we find King Eadred granting the same estate to his minister Ælfsige and Ælfsige's wife, Eadgifu. Two years later Eadred granted 10 hides (1 hide~100 acres) of land at Drayton to Edwold a thegn, and the following year King Eadwig granted East Hanney comprising 20 hides (actual extent 2,119 acres in 1832), to Ælric his adopted father. In 963 King Edgar granted *Hyrde grafe* (Hulgrove) Mill to Æthelsige his clerk at Sparsholt; and in 983 King Ethelred granted land at Drayton (3 hides) and at Sutton to his man Wulfgar; while we know at the time of the Conquest in 1066 King Harold held Steventon.

126

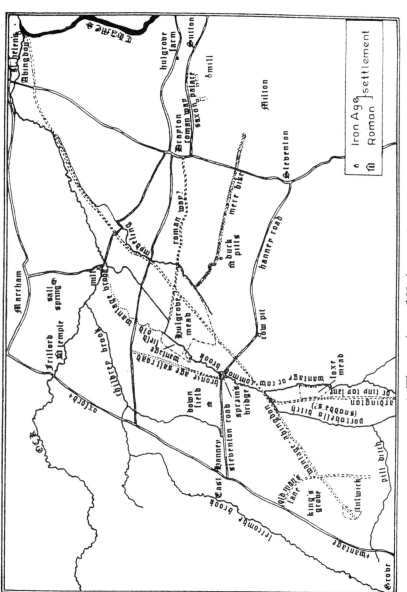

4. The region of Hulgrove Mead.

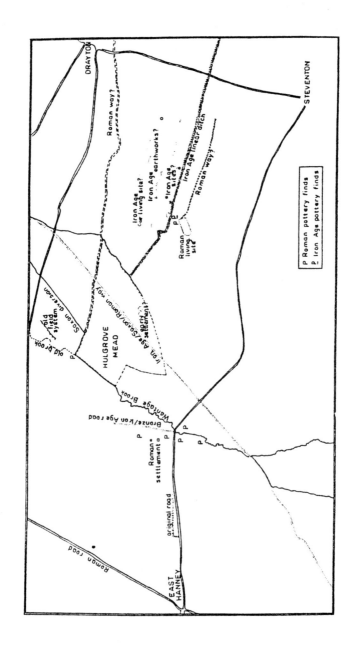

5. Archaeology of the Hulgrove Mead area.

The Puzzle of Hulgrove Meadow

At the heart of the area, the Ordnance Survey Map of 1883 shows the complex arrangement of parish tithes surrounding Hulgrove Meadow through which the ancient army-path runs; a complexity probably evolving from royal ownership in the eighth century. Its northern boundary was probably formed by a Roman way leading east to Drayton. Lying between the parishes of East Hanney, Drayton, and Steventon, Sutton Courtenay township controlled 107 acres of Hulgrove Meadow, and Sutton Wick 58. On its western side Wantage township had 19 acres and West Hendred Parish 4. These Wantage acres, known as "Townlands", were established in an Act of 1597 of Elizabeth I for the proper governing of a charity for the relief of Wantage's poor, repair of its roads and support of its grammar school. The various lands for these purposes were originally donated in the reigns of Henry VI and VII, that is, between 1422 to 1509; thus lands in the royal gift before the dissolution of Abingdon Abbey in 1538.

The name *hyrde graf* or *hirde grafe* means "grove of the shepherds" indicating a woodland, but the word "grove" is also usually associated with a royal preserve. Grove outside of Wantage was once known as King's Grove, belonging to the royal ham at Wantage. *Hyrde graf* is defined in the 1804 Inclosure Map for Sutton as Hulgrove Meadow, an inverted triangle of land looking like a squashed shield in outline, belonging to the Parish of Sutton but isolated within the Parish of Drayton. Formerly royal land, in the fourteenth century Abingdon Abbey owned at least a part of it but seemingly not all, for in 1242 "permanent pasture for twelve oxen" was in private hands as a part of the Caldecott estate. It was held by the king again in the next century.

The north-west corner is marked by a man-made diversion of Wantage Brook, the brook being diverted eastwards approximately one furlong roughly to the centre of the boundary of Hulgrove Meadow, then turning sharply northwards. This diversion was already present in 1760 when John Rocque made his map of the area and probably dates from Anglo-Saxon times, accounting for the tenth century charter referring to "old Wantage Brook" meeting the River Ock, for the former course is still marked by an irregular hedge and ditch forming the parish boundary to this day.

The description of the western boundary of Drayton in 958, which strikes the brook higher up, simply referring to "Wantage", suggests we are back on the original watercourse. It therefore seems highly likely that the brook was diverted to the east before 956, perhaps originally for the mill later apparently granted here to Æthelsige in 963, although the grant may refer to a place in Baulking or to Drayton Mill, Hulgrove Farm in western Sutton Courtenay possibly indicating another Hulgrove in eastern Drayton (3). Experts agree that the Sparsholt charter boundaries are very confusing, but have not considered that they may have originally referred to Sparsholt Court, now East Hendred, which lies to the south of the area.

The references specifying Hulgrove do not refer to this other Hulgrove in western Sutton Courtenay, which would simply fall within the bounds of Sutton. In 1274, for example, when ownership of the manor of Sutton was confirmed for John de Corteney, or Curtenay, the writ states: "The manor... including a pasture called Herdegrave and a member called Hauekerig' [Hawkridge], held of the king in chief as freely as the king held it, and by his charter." Herdegrave is clearly only mentioned by name because it lay outside of the bounds of Sutton. Hawkridge

130

is unidentified apart from one at Bucklebury, near Newbury.

In a charter of 964 in which King Edgar granted land at West Hendred to Abingdon Abbey, an added note states: "The mead which belongs to the 10 hides is on the West side of Wantage". This has been tentatively identified as a 25 acre field anciently known as Foxe Mead lying between present Cow Common Brook and Ardington (Tinytoy) Lane at the north-west extremity of the Parish of West Hendred, now bisected by the railway line. Because this adjunct makes the boundaries very confused the charter has been regarded as suspect, a later invention by the monks in furtherance of a spurious claim. However it is clearly an item tacked on to the end of the main description and the OS Map for 1883 shows an isolated 4 acre field as belonging to West Hendred on the west side of Wantage Brook, south to south-west of the 19 acre Wantage field on the west side of Hulgrove Meadow. Its sinuous southern boundary suggests that this was once the course of the brook at this point and a mill may well have been sited here in proximity to the north-south Bronze Age road, explaining why such a small and irregularly-shaped field was of importance. Hulgrove Meadow may have belonged to Abingdon Abbey at this time as a part of the Sutton estate granted to the Abbey by King Ine in 728, and therefore logical for the Abbey to request the addition of this land on the west, the gift probably encompassing what was later known as "Townlands" and the West Hendred Meadow, a total of just over 24 acres. Hulgrove Meadow was paying tithes to the Abbey in 1274, but the Abbey then only owned a portion of it.

The next grant was East Hanney of which, after the death of Ælric, King Edgar granted 10 hides, or half of the total area, to the Abbey in 968. In 960, possibly on the death of Eadwold, King Edgar had granted the land at Drayton to the Abbey. The further three hides which King Æthelred granted to Wulfgar were then given to the Abbey by the king in the year 1000.

Before the Conquest, of the Abbey's 10 hides in East Hanney, Wulfin had three and Nicholas one. There was one mill. Two free men, one of whom was Godric, had six hides with two mills. Steventon, of 20 hides, was held by King Harold. Two hides in Drayton were also held by King Harold and 3 1/2 by Godwin from King Edward. In Sutton, Leofled held a 1/2 virgate (15 acres), but it was regarded as not belonging in the Sutton revenue and was almost certainly the 15 acre Wantage Field on the west side of Hulgrove Meadow (4).

After the Conquest, at East Hanney the Abbey's holding remained unchanged, but that of the free men was taken by the Count of Evreux who held two hides and Gilbert of Bretteville six. King William took over Steventon's 20 hides, which were then controlled by Roger D'Oilly; while King Harold's land at Drayton was taken by Earl Hugh, and Hascoit Muscard took over the land held by Godwin. King William took over the half-virgate in the Sutton revenue which "does not belong there", according to the domesday book.

Holdings appear to have been grossly under-represented except for Steventon, which had been the dead King Harold's land. These discrepancies could be due to a wide interpretation of what constituted a hide; to the fact that a hide probably only referred to arable land; or that much of the area was not easily accessible and so false returns could be made with impunity.

The land of Steventon never came under Abingdon Abbey, remaining in royal hands until in 1121 it was granted by Henry I to the Prior of Notre Dame du Pr at Rouen, a cell of the Black Monks of the Abbey of Bec in Normandy. A priory only in name, it was not for evangelizing but solely for supplying the material needs of the monks of Le Pré, and would have consisted simply of a manor-house and a chapel. Staffed by a prior and his single companion it sent a small sum annually to Le Pré, averaging 20 marks in 1295. Steventon is distinguished for one of the earliest peasant revolts in England, the tenants in 1288 successfully defending their rights in the courts as sokemen; that is, they were not villeins of the Abbot of Bec but held their land according to certain predetermined services. After a number of viccisitudes the last prior left in 1379 and the following year Hugh de Calvyley obtained custody of Steventon for life from Richard II. In 1399, some time after de Calvyley's death, the king granted it to the Dean and Chapter of Westminster Abbey, which held it until the 19th century.

More About the Cow Road

From Fiveways we struck east, up the road now known as the Steventon Road, passing fields anciently known as Culverhouse, meaning a dovecote; Tinkerbush, perhaps nothing to do with a tinker but referring to ten or tithes; Down, referring to high ground; and Pulbush, the pool-in-the-bushes with reference to Wantage Brook. The division of these fields after the Inclosures, although they were already a mosaic of strips each with its own name, gave us the marvellous hawthorn hedges, now sadly gone for the most part, of which the West Hendred parson's daughter Eleanor Hayden wrote in 1908: "Never have I beheld such masses of May-blossom as are to be found in the lanes of the Vale. It is hard to decide which is the most beautiful - the piled snow-drifts looking ready to fall, the wild parsley that breaks in white foam at their base, or the yellow stretches of buttercup meadows where the cows graze knee-deep."

The road was known until the 'fifties by the older Hanney inhabitants as the "Cow Road", leading to "Cow common"; a reminder of the days before the Inclosures took away the common land. This was really the name of the road out of Steventon, that from Hanney being Sprain's Bridge Way on the Inclosure Map of 1803. Neither name appears on John Rocque's map, nor on the first Ordnance Survey Map of 1830. By Rocque's time the old open field names had already been consigned to oblivion, replaced by the simple "Hanney Field". Common land named Arding-ton Mead is indicated along the boundary stream on the Hanney side, a narrow tongue reaching from the village up on the Downs well south of the area. "Cow Common" only appears on maps after 1830.

In 1839 the "Cow Way" from Steventon terminated at a pond which still exists known as the "Cow Pit" or "Common Pit", dating to before 1483. Now much overgrown it was originally a public watering place with a small copse on its western side called simply *Grafe* or grove, pre-sumably where the cowherds lounged in the shade while their cows watered.

After the Steventon inclosure a metalled road was made connecting that from Hanney to this westbound track from Steventon, the cost of which bankrupted a number of the smaller farmers. The only advantage of this road at the time was an economy in horse power. Whereas previously it had taken three horses to get a load of manure to a given spot in the fields, now one horse could draw the cart along the metalled roadway to a point where a second horse hitched to it would be sufficient to draw the cart across the stiff clay fields.

The brook forming the boundary between the parishes of East Hanney and Steventon known as *"Waneting broc"* and simply waneting, joined by *"Snodda's small stream"*, was probably at land level in Anglo-Saxon times, flowing between reedy marshes, its present deep nature due to continual dredging in modern times. The road crosses it at *"Sprain's Bridge"*, just beyond which is Deadman's Ham on the west side of the road, a name deriving from Old English *dedemersch,* meaning a place that is dead land because it floods. Despite the extensive modern drainage systems and the passage of a thousand years, Deadman's Ham still flooded in January 1995. Although the foregoing therefore seems to be the most likely interpretation of the name, the addition of the word *"ham"*, Old English for a farm, might indicate that a Bronze or Iron Age graveyard was uncovered here in Anglo-Saxon times.

An Ancient salt-Road?

Sprain's Bridge is first mentioned in 1671, so has nothing to do with the construction of the Wilts and Berks Canal or the opening-up of the road. That this remote and swampy crossing was dignified by a bridge seems unusual. Sprain is not a personal name and is possibly a corruption of Old English *spraeg* meaning brushwood: thus bridge in or by a

135

thicket. So why should there have been a bridge here in Anglo-Saxon times? The answer must lie in the fact that a road ran northwards from here as early as late Bronze Age to early Iron Age times. It was bordered by ditches on either side which were filled in during Roman times, perhaps because of an increase in wheeled traffic which tended to slide into the ditches in wet weather. Numerous pottery fragments of Roman date have been found in the area of this road, and some of Iron Age. Perhaps this was a "salt-road", connecting with the salt spring at Marcham, and to the south joining the ancient road from Abingdon which persisted into modern times as the Wantage to Abingdon Bridleway, and along which the old Wilts and Berks Canal was routed. It was also probably joined by the Roman way from Drayton passing along the northern boundaries of Hulgrove Meadow and Wantage Field.

Salt was at a premium in ancient times, used for salting meat and fish for winter storage. Its use has been identified from the Early-Middle Iron Age onwards, but Wessex seemingly witnessed an intensification of production in the later Iron Age, the salt being transported to areas of demand, in earthenware containers. In the early Roman period it became a full-scale industry to supply the growing Roman towns and markets. Most salt works were near the coast, but some counties, such as Cheshire, had numerous inland salt pans in Anglo-Saxon times, marketing the salt though Droitwich. It was essentially a Mercian system, all the manors with known Droitwich links lying in greater Mercia. None is known from Berkshire. Bampton was the nearest known centre to the Vale which had salt rights, but there was a salt market at Shellingford in 1213. Oxford imported at least part of its requirements in the years 700 to 1066 from Droitwich, where it was collected from the Iron Age onwards. No salt industry is recorded from Marcham, but what did exist must have been of great local importance.

There is an inferred salt-way from the Thames at Abingdon, along the Ock to the Roman road at Frilford; but perhaps in fact the traffic was in the contrary direction, from Marcham (*merecehamm* = the riverside meadow where smallage [wild celery] grows) to Abingdon. The Marcham spring presumably did not produce much otherwise there would be some record (unless its location was kept a secret), but it was the only source in the region (5). Abingdon Abbey did not obtain possession of Marcham until 965.

Frilford's importance, with a continuing sacred function from Bronze Age to Roman times, has been put down to a strategic position on the north-south road and control of the upper reaches of the Ock. The real reason may have been its proximity to the Marcham salt spring.

Pagan Shrines and Roman Remains

A Romano-British and early Anglo-Saxon cemetery here contained at least 359 graves, and another theory is that Frilford was probably an Iron Age shrine for worshipping the River Ock itself. In 856 the Ock was described as having its source in The Manger, the precipitous valley just below the head of the White Horse; defined more precisely in 958 as the *occene wyllas* or Ock springs. So perhaps it was regarded as a sacred stream, flowing from this sacred symbol; and there may have been another shrine where it entered the Thames at Abingdon. It has been suggested that the Ock formed the boundary between the Atrebates and the Dobunni, and the two tribes may have met together at Frilford for trade. Perhaps the Atrebates came there to buy Marcham salt.

The first Anglo-Saxons would not have found a Roman temple at Frilford, it would have already been decaying for the century since paganism had been banned. There is no evidence of it being Christianized as were many such shrines in the mid or late fourth century: no church was built there. So perhaps the first Anglo-Saxons resurrected its pagan uses in view of the fact that the brook flowed from the White Horse; but from the mid-fifth century the whole of the Wessex region had become basically Christian.

Halfway between East Hanney and the Steventon parish boundary the site of a Roman villa has been excavated. Two floors were revealed of rough limestone slabs and gravel respectively, but no walls. Some 70 yards to the south were traces of a rectangular building of which the footings of the long walls were located. The building had been 30 feet wide externally and 70 long. A pit containing first century materials was sealed beneath one of the walls. Pottery fragments from the area extended from the first to the third to fourth centuries.

Siting their habitation on the north side of the present main road to Steventon, in the area known until the Inclosures as Down field due to its greater elevation, its occupants probably sought the more open, drier land slightly above the flood plain level of the brook, as well as being close to the Bronze Age road on its east. The road from Hanney may have originally been a Roman road to serve the villa branching off from the Wantage to Frilford road.

Until the canal was constructed the Wantage to Abingdon Bridleway had branches to the villages of West Lockinge and Ardington Wick; and a loop, perhaps a diversion for watering horses, from near Sprain's Bridge upstream along the brook which presumably became Snodda's stream, to the present Hanney Road. Fragments of Roman pottery have been found on the site of this loop road near Snodda's stream.

We saw that the Abingdon to Wantage road was referred to in the 956 charter as the "broad army path", but by 968 had become simply a "narrow way". That the main army-path should virtually disappear in twelve years is very feasible if it was not maintained, but it suggests that the country was not as open as we have been led to believe. We learn from the Chronicle that the warlike King Eadred died in 955 and his son Eadwig who succeeded him died in 959. Eadwig lived in peace and without battle and brought under his sway all that he wished. So perhaps armies had ceased to march to and from Abingdon and Wantage to the Downs.

After 973 the herepaths disappeared altogether replaced by portways, meaning "market ways". Wantage was presumably not sufficiently important as a market town in comparison with Abingdon for this road to continue to have any importance, and the Wantage portway led in only from the nearby villages.

This ancient road which almost bisects the area was probably originally a Bronze Age road, then Iron Age and then Roman; following almost a straight line from the Iron Age valley-fort at the site of St. Helen's Church in Abingdon at the confluence of the Thames and the Ock, to Tulwick near Grove, a settlement of unknown date abandoned in the fifteenth century, and on to Wantage. Almost halfway along its length it connected with the south-north road to Marcham. At the beginning of this century, Wantage's Grove Street was still known as the Abingdon Road and its last building on leaving Wantage was the Abingdon Arms public house, now the only reminder of the road's former ancient connection.

Until the Steventon inclosures, the road from Hanney ended at the loop on the Wantage to Abingdon Bridleway. Travellers had to cross Steventon Common and Steventon Mead before joining the Hanney Road at Cow Pit. Obviously the people of Hanney did not have much in common with those of Steventon in past times, probably due to the latter's former connections with the alien priory. So the direct route to Hanney was from Drayton.

Before Tulwick the road probably branched south along what is now known as Ardington Lane but formerly Tinytoy Lane, a quaint name perhaps a corruption of Old English *tin-tun* or "ten enclosures". Like Tinkerbush perhaps referring to tithe land.

Another odd name in the area is that of Portobello Ditch (formerly Portobello Brook), which rises just north-west of the hamlet of Ardington Wick and appears to have been the original "Wantage Brook" before it was joined by "Snodda's small stream". Perhaps the name derives from *port-bile*, the "market town's bill-like projection", referring to the spur from the Downs to the east of Ardington Wick. Just as the derivation of Portway is considered to be Old English from *port-weg*, "market town road".

On the other hand, Abingdon was the site of a considerable Romano-British settlement, and there was a Romano-British settlement at Limborough, a district in Wantage. Thus perhaps Portobello derives from the Latin "war gate", relating to the track up the valley between the two spurs at Ardington Wick. Maybe in later Anglo-Saxon times Wantage Brook became known as Snodda's along its lower length, and the upper reach had its name changed to *port-bile* to avoid confusion with the new Wanontinge broc (Letcombe Brook). But all this is just speculation. What is certain is that old Wantage Brook does not arise near Wantage, as some authoritioes have stated, but east of Ardington Wick. Pill Ditch (Old English *pyll* = 'small stream'), which now links it to Letcombe Brook, is shown on Rocque's map as having a separate source.

Portobello has been alleged to be an imported foreign name, but if it is the corrupt form of *Puerto bello* (Fine Port) then it must either date from 1502 when Columbus named the site in the Caribbean; or 1596 to commemorate Sir Francis Drake's burial there at sea. Both seem unlikely derivations.

Francis Wise followed the antiquary Salmon who postulated in his "New Survey of England" of 1721, based upon distances between towns given by a Roman writer Antoninus, that Wantage was the site of a Roman town originally called *Glevum*; taken over as their seat by the Anglo-Saxons. Within the memory of living persons Wise stated (1738), Grove Street (known later as Abingdon Road before becoming Grove Street again), like the Faringdon Road, was a hollow way. A road below ground level which could be defended from above. Modern historians tend to dismiss Salmon's idea and most of Wise's views, accepting that *Glevum* was the Roman name for Gloucester.

Abingdon township probably developed as a place of note in the seventh century around Cille's nunnery at Helen-stow. Only much later was an abbey established there, and then not by Hæha (Hean), who was abbot of Bradfield, but by a Mercian Hræthhun, later bishop of Leicester. Easily accessible via the Thames it offered rich pickings and suffered many vicissitudes at the hands of the Danes. By 944 it was desolate, but restored again in 955-9. Perhaps the latter date being a clue to the "broad army path", part of a plan to keep the Danes at bay. Still feared a century after Alfred's death, their ravages were to continue

141

until 1006, when they ransacked the Abbey for the last time.

An Iron Age Relic

John Rocque's map shows, in addition to the ancient road from Abingdon to Wantage, another significant road or track bearing due west along the boundary between the parishes of Drayton and Steventon. In 1761 it ended at Mydeling Brook, but probably originally joined with the Abingdon road.

The deep ditch which runs along much of its former length, still retains the name of Mere Dike from the Old English *mær dic* for boundary ditch. Pottery remains show that there was Iron Age habitation near the dike, suggesting that it was constructed either then or earlier in the later Bronze Age, to provide a line of demarcation between two tribal areas, known today as Drayton and Steventon after their later Anglo-Saxon names. Bordering the ditch the ground is markedly raised on the north side, indicating there was originally a raised bank along its length. It has been assumed that the dike was for drainage into Ginge Brook to the east, but the land falls westwards two metres along its length, so if it was for conducting water then it was more likely to be for bringing it from Ginge Brook to Mydeling Brook.

Linear ditches on the Downs date from as late as 800 BC, six major linear ditches dividing the Down land into distinct blocks based on the Lambourn River. Little is known of their function but it probably involved the re-arrangement of settlement patterns and may have marked boundaries between different groups. Such Iron Age ditches which demarcated these fields, or remains of them, are rare in the Thames Valley, Mere Dike perhaps being one of the few surviving examples. Aerial photographs show a number of circular crop marks north of the ditch which may indicate former Iron Age huts or enclosures. There is also the appearance of terraces or earthworks characteristic of causewayed enclosures of the Bronze Age, present on the ground as low ridges, perhaps long ago reduced almost to ground level. The track from Drayton to Mydeling, following an ancient east-west route, mirrors a kink in one of the possible earthworks, suggesting that the track originally followed a raised bank.

Near the termination of the dike many fragments of Roman pottery have been found. Most finds centre on a field known as Duck Pitts, perhaps a corruption of Dike Pits (Old Englkish *dic-pytts*) signifying former pits in the ground near the dike. The Roman pottery, and a number of Roman *tegulae* or roof tiles, show that there was a typical 3rd to 4th century occupation site here, and from the air a rectangular crop mark is visible perhaps indicating a former villa. Settled from pre-Roman through to Roman times, perhaps it began as a Bronze Age or Iron Age settlement based on the small stream to the west, now no more than a ditch at this point, known in Anglo-Saxon times as *mydelinge* or "stream". It is significant that *mydelinge* is possibly one of the rare Bronze to Iron Age name survivals. A clue to the choice of site may lie in an old field name in the area, "Red Pitts Furlong", the field characterised by red ferruginous clay probably favoured for pot-making.

Field Names of the Past

A map of unenclosed Steventon drawn up in 1839 names all of the fields in the area, the majority of which is of Anglo-Saxon origin, but none indicates a former settlement. A large group was named Great, Lower Little and Upper Middle Hinge Furlong: "Hinge" possibly a corruption meaning "land belonging to a manorial servant or workman" (*enche* = Old English 'manorial servant or workman'). farther east the word 'inch' is retained in Upper and Lower Inch Land. Also in the area of the former settlement were the western ends of Upper and Lower Stone Furlong, not uncommon names usually relating to a stone marking the end of the furlong. At the western side of Steventon parish was Ealing Furlong, 'ealing' referring to an eel-fishery based on Wantage Brook. Next to which was the enclosed wood for the deer to provide the provender for Steventon Priory; which later became a field known as The Been, perhaps a corruption of the word 'boon' with reference to manorial custom, an unpaid service due by a tenant to his lord. So perhaps the field, in the extreme west of the parish, had to be ploughed by tenants without payment.

Old Drayton field names for the area are of no help either in establishing sites of former settlements. In those on a 1789 map Meer Ditch Furlong becomes Tuckwell Furlong (probably a personal name); then Innmeer Furlong (meaning wet land near the brook taken into an estate by clearing). North of these fields, from west to east is Short Hale, Long Hale, Hank Furlong Heads and Rush Pit Furlong. Hale probably stems from Old English *healh*, meaning 'corner', for above it lies Hulgrove Corner. Hank is perhaps a corruption of hangra, meaning a meadow. 'Heads' is a common name referring to a headland where the plough turned, and Rush Pit speaks for itself.

No map of the old field system for East Hanney is known to survive, but it has been possible to determine the whereabouts of some names mentioned in early manorial documents. The field in which the Bronze Age road occurs has only one likely connection in a field termed "in the Breach" (*bræc* = Old English 'land broken up for cultivation'). The location of Wick Furlong in Down Field has not been determined but probably relates to the former Roman building there, (*wic* = Old English 'dwelling' or 'farm').

Why were the settlements both east and west of the brook abandoned? On the Steventon side, when the land came under the Abbey of Bec, the prior may have had the residents brought in close to Steventon so that he could keep an eye on them, for the alien priories were viewed with suspicion and isolated settlements might have fomented trouble. Indeed we have seen that the Steventon people stood up against the prior in claiming their rights. This may have also accounted for the severing of contact with the Bronze Age road to Marcham, leading to its disuse; as well as the road to Hanney which was not to be re-opened for another 780 years. This could have accounted for any settlement disappearing without leaving a trace of its name. As did that on the Hanney side and perhaps others in the vicinity of Hulgrove Meadow.

Only two ancient (circa 1242) field names for Hulgrove Meadow can be traced: lincham and linchakar. These names may refer to strips of land, the former by a river meadow boundary, the latter simply "boundary acre", deriving from Old English *hlinc* - a ridge or boundary.

This apparently uninteresting expanse of flat fields under its present intensive cultivation, conceals a treasure trove of historic knowledge for the inquisitive historian. Follow the bridleway from near to where Hanney's "Old

Man's Lane" ("the King's Boundary") meets the railway, diagonally across along the line of the old canal, through Hulgrove Meadow on to New Cut Mill (Sutton Wick or Bug's Mill) and to St. Helen's Church where Cille built her nunnery, and you are treading a road used since the Bronze Age, along which Roman legions then marched, and Anglo-Saxon warriors after them.

Hulgrove could have been associated with an Anglo-Saxon palace, and we know that there was considerable settlement from pre-Roman times both east and west of it. On its west was Wantage Field. Could this, then, have been the site of a former Wantage and the real birthplace of King Alfred?

Notes

1. Alfred was alleged to have owned Appleford in Berkshire, which he exchanged for land which has been identified as Horn Down in East Hendred. Since it is not mentioned in his will the charter is regarded with some suspicion but he may have traded the land away since it would be a relatively small piece.

2. The 968 East Hanney Charter read: "First to the old dike and then the headstumps [posts on which the heads of beheaded criminals were exposed]. Along the dike to wantage [brook]. Then along stream to the red pool then cilla's brook. Then at that point it goes east. Then along stream till it runs into the Ock. Then along the Ock till it

runs into the old wantage [brook]. Then it goes west along stream till it runs into Snodda's small stream. Then it goes west to the headland [end of a ploughing strip] till it comes to the narrow way. Then along the way till it goes again to the old dike."

3. At whichever of these sites it may have been, the mill had apparently disappeared by the time of the Domesday Survey. In the eastern counties many mills disappeared between 1066 and 1087, perhaps reflecting a continuing country-wide decline.

4. Leofled appears to have been a churchman living in Wallingford.

5. A 19th century description of the spring is given in Druce, 1897.

Chapter 6

King Alfred's Real Birthplace?

Old Wantage and the Grove of the Shepherds

> Wherefore these courts are in decay and these
> lofty gates; the woodwork of the roof is
> stripped of tiles; the place has sunk into ruin,
> levelled to the hills, where in times past many
> a man light of heart and bright with gold,
> adorned with splendours, proud and flushed
> with wine, shone in war trappings, gazed on
> treasure, on silver, on precious stones, on
> riches, on possessions; on costly gems, on this
> bright castle of the broad kingdom.
>> Anglo-Saxon poem "The Ruin".

The Anomaly of Abingdon Abbey

Alfred could have been born somewhere within less than
nine miles of Abingdon Abbey. Although the Abbey had its
origins in the late eighth century or the beginning of the
ninth, as a minster of modest structure twenty feet in length
tended only by an abbott and twelve monks; by the time of
Alfred's birth we may suppose that it had expanded into
something more significant.

Romano-British finds at Abingdon suggest a substantial
settlement had existed at this confluence of the rivers
Thames and Ock, with its adjacent Andersey Island, prior

148

to the early Anglo-Saxon occupation. Neolithic pits of Stone Age Man, Bronze Age barrows and a settlement dating from 800 BC in the Iron Age, as well as Roman remains, bear witness to the enduring popularity of this site.

Fact and fiction are inextricably interwoven in the history of the Abbey's foundation spawning an involved tracery of romantic images entangled in time, and the recorded early history may in fact refer to the lost minster of Bradfield, near Reading, established about 670, and which was endowed with the great estate of Earmundesleah (the woodland of Ærmund) around Appleton in the bend of the River Thames. After Bradfield disappeared, perhaps destroyed by the Danes, its charters seem to have come into the possession of the monks of Abingdon, who believed them to relate to their own abbey.

One of the witnesses to the endowment charter was a lady by the name of Æbbe, hence perhaps bbe's dun or hill=Abingdon. There was also a small Anglo-Saxon church in Oxford of St. Ebbe, and a village street called Ebb's Lane in East Hanney may have some ancient connection.

But Abingdon is not on a hill and Abbandun was a name given to a part of Boar's Hill just south of Oxford ('boar' here being a corruption of barrow). The Chronicles refer to the abbey moving from a hill to a lowland site previously called Seovechesham. The name Seacourt in Oxford is derived from Seofecanwyrthe, a similar name in the region which may derive from a property-owning Romano-Briton named Sevecus or Scibbio. There is no indication of what Abingdon may have been called in Roman times. Although there may have been a nunnery there from the seventh century as we have seen, Abingdon Abbey was a Mercian foundation, begun by the Mercian

149

abbot Hræthhun, and not, as was originally believed, a West Saxon foundation.

The twelfth-century chronicler who lived there waxed eloquent of its beauty: "A famous city, fair to the eye, full of wealth, surrounded by rich fields, blossoming meadows and far-stretching pastures with milk-bearing kine." But that was long after.

According to tradition it was based upon a grant of land in 675 from the West Saxon underking Cissa, who is otherwise completely unknown, to his nephew Hæha, later mistakenly rendered Hean, a West Saxon nobleman; together with Hæha's sister Cille. Cille has been now identified as a member of the family who were the proprietors of Bradfield. Hæha moved the Abbey to its later position in the time of Caedwealh after the destruction of the cell of Bradfield. The year 675 may have simply reflected the Abingdon chronicler's unwillingness to admit the seniority of a rival establishment, for it was in that year that the Mercian King Wulfhere installed a bishop at Dorchester. From then onwards Abingdon and Dorchester belonged to different kingdoms and different dioceses.

The story continues that Hæha did nothing with the land at first and it was confiscated by King Ine. Sometime just prior to 709 Ine restored the land to Hæha and Cille, Hæha then took the vows to become an abbot and began his small monastery. But all this referred to Bradfield and meanwhile, not later than 816 and perhaps in 801, a monastery was established at Abingdon under Hrtæhhun, later bishop of Leicester. Hæha never was abbot there and the land was more likely a gift from Coenwulf (d.819), the Mercian king, than a gift from Ine. Perhaps its establishment was the reason why Cille moved her nunnery to Wytham.

150

Situated as it was, the monastery became a kind of shuttlecock between the kings of Mercia and Wessex, Egbert's triumph over Mercia being short-lived, until it was destroyed by the Danes in 871. But the wily monks had sufficient warning to flee with their charters and relics and hide them. As to the monastery, although nothing but the walls were left it appears to have soon been re-inhabited but was deserted in 954 when King Eadred gave it to Æthelwold.

An obscure tradition relates that at the time of the attack on Abingdon, the abbot sent a party from the monastery to one of two defensive camps outside of the town; either one to the north-east (Barrow Hills), or to the west (Barrow Farm area); a support which helped the defenders to vanquish the Danes, and perhaps thereby prevent a westward advance. For this the Abbey was allegedly given lands. The opposite was the reality, that the Abbey lost lands after this attack, suggesting perhaps the abbot did not help in the defence of Abingdon.

A number of the early charters later put forward by the Abbey as evidence for its land holdings south of the Thames are believed by some to have been fraudulent documents issued by Mercian kings in attempts to regain control south of the river, but this belief seems largely due to failure to appreciate the confusion between Bradfield and Abingdon. From 733 to 752 the area was ruled by the Mercian King Æthelbald until he was defeated by Cuthred at Burford. But in 777 Offa re-took Benson and the area was brought back under Mercian control. It was probably more than twenty years after this that Abingdon Abbey was founded. As late as 844 Beorhtwulf possessed Berkshire through the Mercian ealdorman Æthelwulf, but Alfred's birth south of the Thames suggests that this area, or at least

151

a part of it, had come under the jurisdiction of the West Saxon bishops by 849.

As the area had been under Mercian rule, it is unlikely that Alfred's mother would have spent long in the region before his birth. We can only speculate that the region had become strategically important to prevent the Danes using the Downs to penetrate westwards into Wessex, and leading to the royal household moving to the area from farther west after 843 when Æthelwulf was in Somerset.

Wessex kings may have retained their estates in the region when it fell under Mercian rule, although this supposition has been regarded by one authority as "bizarre" (1). A Mercian ealdorman was in charge of Berkshire, and the final recovery of the shire does not seem to have taken place until 853 when Burhred requested Æthelwulf's help against the north Welsh. To further the alliance he married Æthelwulf's daughter Æthelswyth. Three years later Æthelwulf granted land at Ashbury to one of his thegns, suggesting perhaps that the cession of Berkshire may have been the price of his assistance to Burhred. Although in 868 Æthelswyth granted to her thegn Cuthred an estate at Lockinge, so she had kept her Berkshire possessions despite her Mercian marriage.

The first grant of land in our area made to Abingdon Abbey may have been that of Hulgrove Meadow as a part of the vill of Sutton. Tradition has it that King Ine granted Sutton to the Abbey between 688 and 728, but there is no charter to support the claim. Sutton always remained a royal vill apart from a small estate belonging to the monastery. In 801 one hundred *manentes* of land were allegedly given to King Cynewulf of the Mercians with a payment of £120 for Andersey Island. According to tradition, this island, which was in Mercia, had belonged to the Abbey as part of Cissa's gift, but was obtained in exchange for Goosey by the Mercian king Offa, who intended to build a royal residence there because he was so charmed by the tranquil scene. In reality he probably wanted it for its strategic importance, Abingdon becoming the southern limit of his annexations.

His son Egfrid built a palace on the island and subsequently used it as a hunting lodge, keeping hounds and hawks there. The baying of the hounds became a great annoyance to the Abbey and so in 801 the abbot negotiated to buy the island back again. Then in 844 Ceolred, bishop of Leicester, gave the Mercian king Beorhtwulf 14 hides of land at Pangbourne in order to secure the freedom of "certain monasteries". This almost certainly included Abingdon because the document was preserved there. Thus from 844 Abingdon Abbey would have claimed freedom of all of its lands from royal ownership.

This brings us to the mystery connecting Alfred with Abingdon. Soon after his victory at the battle of Ashdown in 871 and after he became king, he plundered the Abbey, taking away "violently" the township of Abingdon and most of the Abbey's other landed possessions. One of the monks writing in the early twelfth century records: "After the death of King Æthelred his brother Alfred assumed power. He alienated the vill in which the monastery is placed which is commonly called by the name of Abbandun, with all its appurtenances from the said monastery, rendering to the victorious Lord an unequal return for the victory with which he was endowed." Another chronicler is more outspoken, alleging that Alfred added evil to evil, acting "like Judas amongst the Twelve".

Why did Alfred thus treat the Abbey of Abingdon? It was completely out of character with all else that we were

153

once led to believe of him but now know to be an impression largely initiated by Alfred himself. It has been argued that it would have been perfectly logical for Alfred to take control of the area after the attack, someone who was able to organise its defences, and that it was only a small monastery anyway. It has also been argued that it was normal procedure for monastic lands to return to royal control after an abbot's death, and one chronicler indeed states that Alfred took the lands upon Abbot Alhard's death. Ælfric of Eynsham in his "Life of St. Ethelwold" (c1010) accepted it as a matter of course. But can the matter be so lightly dismissed?

It is an episode conveniently omitted in almost all the lives which have been written of King Alfred; all versions of "Asser's". If it is mentioned, Alfred is given the benefit of the doubt. It has been suggested that the monks, writing three centuries after the event, wanted to give the sanction of ancient possession to their tenure of the whole of Abingdon. Yet in the great charter of Æthelred of 993 occurs a statement which suggests an unlawful action on Alfred's part, when, after describing the restoration of Abingdon Abbey by Kings Eadred, Eadwig and Eadgar, the charter reads "...the aforesaid kings, restoring to the Church of God the estate which is called Abingdon....in which our predecessors, deceived with devilish avarice, had unjustly built a royal building for themselves, forbade that any king should require entertainment there or raise a building at any time."

It has been argued that Alfred had to strip the monasteries in order to find sufficient funds to pay off the Danes the enormous amounts which they demanded, selling the lands to his thegns (one wonders how they had the money to buy the estates). Yet as far as we know there had been no West Saxon treaties with the Danes up to this date and no treaty after Ashdown, although if there had been a need for funds after Ashdown, Abingdon would have been the nearest monastery for Alfred to plunder. There may have been a treaty after Wilton, or later in the year, for Alfred bought them off, i.e. "made peace with them" in the words of the Chronicle, before the end of the year. But the coffers could not have been empty at the beginning of the year. Even if they had been the charter of Æthelred implies that Alfred kept the Abingdon property for his own use, but Smyth has argued that Alfred used the situation to benefit himself, a mean opportunist seizing estates on the pretext that he required the money to pay the Danes (1), an explanation which would imply a very bad start to Alfred's reign.

The chronicle of John of Brompton contains an obscure passage for the year 871 in which Alfred is defeated in a battle at a place called Abendune as well as at Chippenham (the known battle at Chippenham was in 878). As these events do not fit in with other records, they are generally ignored, but that does not mean to say that they did not take place. Had Alfred, the newly-crowned king, attempted to repulse the Danes' attack on Abingdon and dissatisfied with the backing of the monastery, exacted vengeance upon it? After all, Abingdon was on the border of Mercia and perhaps the abbot felt that it was safer to sit on the fence, especially as he was probably a Mercian. Who would protect it when Alfred was absent? Would the Mercian king?

Then there are the interpolations in "Asser's" biography which tend to depict Alfred as a weakling or tyrant. Most important is the sentence: "For when he began to reign, as he was yet a young man, he was given up to youthful

155

passions, and when the men of the realm subject to him came to him and sought his aid and favour, he would neither hear them nor give any help to them, but utterly despised them." There was probably more to it than an attempt to portray him as a "third-rate mediaeval saint", rather after Æthelred's charter the monks felt able to express their grievances concerning his treatment of Abingdon, albeit by oblique references as Alfred was already an honoured legend and allegory and hidden meanings were common in mediaeval writing.

We have seen that there was a long-running dispute between the kings of Wessex and Mercia concerning the lands to the west of the middle Thames which probably had a bearing on Alfred's actions. It is the contract between bishop Ceolred and Beorhtwulf which Alfred seems to have violated because it was a Mercian agreement. The vill of Abingdon still appears to have been in royal hands in 926 for King Athelstan held court there that Easter, unless he was paying homage to the Abbey. We know it was in royal hands in King Eadred's time, and when Abbot Ethelwold undertook charge of the decayed monastery sometime after 948 it had only 40 hides of land, the rest being held by the king by virtue of office.

It has been argued that the boundary between Mercia and Wessex must have been settled by 849 because of Alfred's birth at Wantage, and therefore Berkshire must have been transferred to Wessex by that date. But there is no entry for such an important event in the Chronicle. It is in 853 that we have evidence of negotiations between Mercia and Wessex, and only from 860 onwards is it definite that Berkshire was a part of Wessex.

Despite the possibility that Alfred may have been born close to the Abbey, not once is the Abbey mentioned in his

156

reign in the Chronicle. The first reference in the Chronicle is in the year that one of the copies of the manuscript ends, 977, when King Edward ordered that the body of Bishop Sideman of Devonshire be conveyed to Abingdon and buried in St. Mary's monastery. The original Chronicle is believed to have been begun about 890, and two copies of it made at Abingdon in the late tenth century. It is surprising therefore that interpolations of a local flavour were not inserted into the Abingdon copies.

If not at Abingdon, then where did the young Alfred seek his spiritual instruction, and who baptised him? Where did his mother Osburh seek her spiritual confessor, and where did she seek her churching after his birth? We have no record of Alfred's birth in the Anglo-Saxon Chronicle for there are no entries from 845 to 851. It would have been logical for the royal family to have been established near to an abbey while the king was absent fighting, for although the royal courts were regarded as itinerant, without a permanent base, there are no references to the Anglo-Saxon kings taking their wives into the field with them. Wives and mistresses are more likely to have occupied permanent residences where they received and entertained the kings on their travels, as is shown by the story of the murder of Cynewulf.

Nothing links present Wantage with Abingdon at this time. The only tenuous link of Alfred with Abingdon is that in 868, when he was 19 years old, he put his name as one of the witnesses to the document in which his sister, Queen Æthelswyth of Mercia, granted land at Lockinge to her minister Cuthwulf, who subsequently gave the land to the monastery. The document was also witnessed by King Burghred of Mercia and Alfred's brother Æthelred, King of Wessex (2). Although Abbot Alhard of Abingdon also put

157

his hand to it, it may not have been signed there. We shall see how Billingsgate fish matters were decided at Wantage. Such things were dealt with by the kings on circuit wherever they might be. It does show, however, that in spite of past enmities the West Saxons and the Mercians were not now hostile to one another.

Alfred's ignoring Abingdon Abbey while apparently showing great commitment to the Church could have one of several interpretations. Perhaps he chose to ignore it because it was a Mercian institution, or the problem may have been Abingdon's position in the centre of the border tussle between the Mercians and the West Saxons. Andersey Island, which both the Abbey and Anglo-Saxon royalty claimed, lay in Mercia, while the Abbey may have been in the West Saxon kingdom. Or perhaps Alfred's actions were the continuation of a vendetta, his aim being to weaken the influence of Abingdon by creating other abbeys. Alternatively he may have been acting in atonement for the wrongs he had done the Abbey, but if so, then why did he totally ignore the place which he had wronged? He would be more likely to have made some gesture towards it than omit all mention. Alfred allegedly gave a part of his income to certain monasteries but Abingdon is not mentioned in this connection. And in his dooms any guilty person who fled to a monastery which received the king's "food-rent", or "some other privileged community which is worthy of this honour", was granted sanctuary for three days. Abingdon, it seems, did not qualify for this privilege.

The only reference to Alfred and Abingdon comes in the early twelfth century Abingdon chronicles, the *Chronicon Monasterii de Abingdon*, when he is alleged to have seized the Abbey's landed possessions. A reference which most historians have preferred to either ignore or gloss over.

158

Alfred's Grudge

The only concession that Alfred apparently made towards Abingdon, if we can believe the charter as genuine, was that towards the end of the ninth century he allowed his minister Deormod to leave five hides of land at Appleford to the Abbey in the event of Deormod's death; land which Alfred had exchanged with Deormod for some at East Hendred.

The Abbey was ransacked by the Danes, but then why was it left to Edward, Alfred's son, to restore back to the Abbey the churches of Wickham and Cumnor which Alfred had taken away; and appoint an abbot, or at least someone to take charge, Cynath?

Clearly Alfred bore a grudge against Abingdon Abbey, perhaps related to the time when with his family he may have been forced to abandon "old Wantage". Let us suppose, for we have no evidence of the fact, that his mother had been living in the royal residence on Andersey Island, close by the Abbey, a most probable situation that a devout queen would want to adopt for her daily prayers and to have her confessor nearby. Even if it were a Mercian abbey let us not forget that her daughter married the Mercian king in 852. Although the island belonged in effect to the Abbey by virtue of its purchase by the abbot from the Mercians in 801, it was still in Mercian territory. But it is possible that this was not recognised by Æthelwulf who took over the former Mercian royal residence, perhaps claiming that it had been ceded to his Berkshire territory as the Abbey itself was in his territory. He then installed his family there to stake his claim. But after Ceolred's agreement with the Mercian king in 844, while the king was away fighting in the west country, the queen and her household were forced by the abbot to leave, and so moved just outside of Abingdon to near Hulgrove, which was still in the king's hand. Here, five years later, Alfred was born. In a vill by the side of Wantage Brook. Let us then suppose that when the Danes ransacked Abingdon in 871 this was too close for comfort, they were only four miles distant along the broad army path. So Alfred's mother and her household, perhaps also Alfred himself and his wife, then fled in the opposite direction five miles along the highway to a fortified position in the lime trees - Limborough, later known as Wantage.

If such a sequence of events were true, Alfred could have harboured a grudge against the Abbey, a desire to restore "loss of face" for fancied wrong to his mother. Revenge for wrongs in the shape of feuds was an established custom in Anglo-Saxon life (3). So at the earliest opportunity, after he became king, he went back down the highway to Abingdon and "pillaged" it.

Spending much of his later life in atonement by supporting the Church, although he later engaged bishops, priests, and monks, to assist him in his scholarship and his attempt to revive monasticism, Abingdon Abbey, so close to the "royal residence" of Wantage, is never mentioned. It was to be fifty years after Alfred's death before King Æthelstan kept Easter with his full court there.

What made Alfred so incensed with the Abbey that while there were battles to be fought against the Danes on all sides, he took time off after defeat at the second battle at Reading (or it may have been the battle of Meretun), to hurry to Abingdon and plunder the Abbey before dashing off to fight one month later at Wilton, west of Newbury?

It has been suggested that it was necessary to secure it for defence, but this would not have necessitated taking away its rights over lands.

Was Alfred perhaps furious with the abbot because he had tried to collaborate with the Danes? This seems improbable if it is true that the abbot sent people to help defend one of the defensive camps outside Abingdon, vanquishing the Danes. Or, had the monks told the Danes the whereabouts of the royal village just four miles away, the reason why Alfred had to abandon "old Wantage"? Or did he wait until he was king to avenge the expulsion of his family from Andersey before his birth?

These are puzzles of the past the answers to which we shall never know. What is certain is that the statement that Wantage was Alfred's birthplace "is in fact indisputable" (4) is, on the contrary, very much open to question.

Wantage

Wantage, a small and thankfully rather quiet market town, its square dominated by a statue of King Alfred with the face of Lord Wantage and crown imaginary (5); was built on the site of a large Romano-British settlement where the Cunetio (Mildenhall) road crossed the ancient Ridgeway road, ancient already at the time of the Romans. Smyth (1) believes that Wantage was almost certainly in Mercian hands up to within three or four years of Alfred's birth, a Mercian no-man's land which lay well south of Abingdon thus implying that Abingdon was well and truly Mercian.

A town is not mentioned here in Domesday, nor is there any evidence from late Anglo-Saxon mints of Wantage being a town or market, unlike the nearby Saxon royal town of Faringdon where Edward the Elder died in 924 and which has Domesday urban connections. And places like Marcham and Sutton Courtenay with explicit Domesday links. Neither was Wantage the site of an early Anglo-Saxon minster; unlike its near neighbours Abingdon, Marcham, Faringdon and Bampton. Not until the ninth or tenth century was a minster or mother church apparently installed there; that is, a church on a royal estate responsible for a district. But "Asser's" simple statement that Alfred was born in the royal residence at a place called Wantage has become enlarged into such statements as "King Alfred of blessed memory was born in the palace of the Kings of Wessex at Wantage." Would there not have been a minster here if that were true? We have only "Asser's" statement that Alfred was born at Wantage and one has to admit that, writing a century after Alfred's death, if the pseudo-biographer did not even know the name of Alfred's queen (as was the case), then it is most unlikely that he would have known where Alfred was born. So one could conjecture that he consulted Alfred's will and chose the most obscure place that he could find in it, Wantage, the royal estate Alfred bequeathed to his wife. "Asser" could have chosen the adjoining Lambourn, it was five times the size but worth somewhat less. We have to set against this the fact that Æthelred summoned a *witan* at Wantage in 990 and again in 997, when he issued an important code of laws there, about the period when "Asser" is believed to have written his Life. So perhaps Wantage was not so obscure after all.

Smyth argues that Wantage could not have been Alfred's birthplace because it was too close to Mercian territory, if not in it. He argued that Æthelwulf would not have left his pregnant queen so close to Mercian hands, "It flies in the face of common sense, poses real historical problems..". But an alliance of sorts had existed between Mercia and Wessex since the 840s, and Mercian dependance on Wessex is clear from 853. The impression is, by this time at least, the West Saxons and the Mercians were not implacable enemies. Disputes arose, but on the whole they co-operated with one another and wherever possible sought intermarriage to strengthen the bond. Insecurity could be said to have existed almost anywhere, but the Danes' assault on the upper Thames region was not until 871. The area had been untouched by them until they reached Abingdon when Alfred was by then in his twenties. Thus near to Abingdon was, in 847-8, probably as safe a place as anywhere for the king's wife.

Alfred has been credited with setting up the system of fortress towns or "burhs" in which everyone within 25 miles could take refuge with his family and some of his property when a Danish raiding party was in the area. These already existed before his birth, but he developed a number of new ones. The West Saxon system was to divide the kingdom into administrative districts termed *regiones*, and within each *region* the central place was a *burh* or defended house, the centre of a royal estate or *villa regalis* controlled by the king's reeve. Such would have been the "palace" of Wantage if Wantage had been a *burh*, but it was not listed in the Burghal Hidage (6). In Wessex a *villa regalis* was to be found on average every six to eight miles.

Wallingford on the Thames was Berkshire's main *burh*. Reading also was a *burh*, as was the Mercian Oxford. It has been shown that where the sites of *burhs* were more than 16 acres in their original area, reflecting the plans of the king for his site, the *burh* was intended as a town, fortified, but a centre of commerce as well as a military garrison. These continued in this role appearing in the Domesday Survey as a borough. But if the area were less than 16 acres in extent, then the intention was to have a fort, a purely military establishment. These forts all disappear before Domesday. Wantage therefore appears to have been simply one of

163

many a *villa regalis* planned as a fort, accounting for the few Saxon remains which have been found there and the fact that it had disappeared as a town by Domesday, possessing only one mill, a church, and 84 people. "Asser" referred to it as a *villa regia*. Stone buildings were called *villae regiae*.

Alfred's alleged establishment of a Court school for the education of the sons of his upper classes is yet another myth. King Alfred's School at Wantage probably had its origin in 1434, existing in some form or another until 1832 when, as a grammar school, it fell into disuse. It was revived in 1849 as a part of the commemoration of the milleniary of Alfred's birth, unashamedly adopting the motto *Alfredus Rex Fundator*, King Alfred the Founder. But Alfred never did found a school at Wantage; just as he never founded the University of Oxford.

Wantage lacks any evidence to suggest that it was a place of note. It is doubtful whether Alfred spent much time there, if any, after he became king. A king did not regularly visit all of his villae regales, some perhaps were never visited at all. They were more like farms, storing the produce until the king and his retinue required it, either there or elsewhere. The reeve had to defend these stores against theft and pillaging, perhaps the origin of their fortifications.

That Wantage was of relatively minor importance is attested by the fact that he bequeathed it in his will to his wife, Ealhswith. As he himself explained in his will, it had been the custom to bequeath property in the male line. His grandfather bequeathed his lands on the spear-side, not on the spindle-side, as Alfred put it. Thus if he gave any that he had acquired to anyone on the female side, his kinsmen were to make compensation. His provision implied that when Ealhswith died the property should revert to a male heir. Hence in 955 King Eadred owned Wantage and much of the surrounding country, bequeathing it to his mother; and it is perhaps from this time that Wantage increased in some importance. We know that Æthelred summoned a witan there in 990 discussing such business affairs as the tolls to be paid for landing fish at Billingsgate; and seven years later while sitting in judgement there he issued a code of laws, Wantage being referred to as a vill. It was to be Domesday before it was mentioned again.

That Æthelred summoned a crowd of bishops, earls, and the highest nobles, has been interpreted as showing that Wantage was a town of considerable size and repute to be able to accomodate such a concourse. But the kings and their courts were itinerant, and their accomodation would probably have been simple thatched, wooden, or wattle and daub, huts.

Wantage came to Alfred through Æthelwulf's will. Before his death in January 858 Æthelwulf made a will in which he provided for the poor and the church and he willed that his kingdom should remain divided between his two sons, Æthelbert receiving Kent and Æthelbald the West Saxon kingdom. If Æthelbald should die childless, as was to be the case, then the rule was to pass to Æthelred and Alfred in succession. His estates he divided between his sons, daughter, and other kindred. Wantage probably went to Alfred at this time; and perhaps Sutton also. On all his estates Æthelwulf ordered that one poor man in ten, whether native or foreigner, should be fed and clothed by his successors until the man's death. A condition of tenure was that the land should be inhabited by men and cattle and not be allowed to lie fallow. The will also stipulated an annual sum of money for Rome. Wantage's status as a royal vill is not in doubt, for the adjacent Charlton signifies a tun occupied by ceorls or peasant farmers. They were probably

165

not free men but belonged to the king, Charltons often being found next to royal centres and probably were the source of supplies for the royal table.

Wantage appears to have been *bocland,* land which might be held by freemen of all ranks and degrees. It was distinct from *folcland,* the property of the community, either occupied in common or parts were assigned to individuals by the court of the district but could not be alienated in perpetuity, returning to common land upon expiration of the term for which it had been granted. *Bocland,* as a private estate of the king, did not merge in the crown but was divisible by will, gift, sale or inheritance. Bestowed on a third party, on the condition of reversion, it became *laenland* (loan-land), and from Alfred's will it would appear that Wantage became *laenland* as it had to revert to the male line upon the death of Ealhswith. She herself could not bequeath it as she would. *Bocland* bequeathed to females was considered as given only in usufruct, that is for temporary use, and reverted to the male line. Not until the fifth generation could *bocland* fall unrestricted from the male side to that of the female. To suppose that Wantage was not *bocland* would have meant that four generations possessed it before Alfred. That is, it would have had to have been held by Eafa about 718, but it may well have been owned two generations before this by Ine in the seventh century.

There is some evidence to suggest that the north slopes of the Downs initially belonged to the royal vill of Wantage and that it was probably once a much larger estate later subdivided by the land being given away. But this would also suggest that it was not a place of importance, unlike the royal vill with a minster church of Lambourn immediately to the south, which remained intact. The areas given away may have been those of only medium pro-

166

sperity and appendant to, but not immediately adjacent to, royal territory. Their parallel, longitudinal shapes, relate to the streams which they bordered.

Nothing of note has been found at Wantage, but both Drayton and Sutton Courtenay had impressive groups of large rectangular timber buildings set out in L-shaped linear formation, probably after AD 600. These places may have been occupied by chiefs or subkings rather than kings, and may be loosely called "palaces". There was a royal Anglo-Saxon villa just over one and a half miles south-east of Drayton. This Drayton palace settlement overlay a neolithic cursus and three Bronze Age barrows. So the early Anglo-Saxons chose these ancient sites to settle on, perhaps because of the materials already there, or because the Neolithic peoples had selected the driest and best areas. Or perhaps for religious reasons, as a form of ancestral reverence. From the later sixth century they started to use Roman sites.

Old Wantage

As Cow Common Brook was known in the tenth century as Wantage Brook, and a West Hendred charter refers to a field "on the west side of Wantage", the site of an original Wantage vill may have been in the vicinity of this brook. That being so, the region of Hulgrove Meadow, an appurtenance of Sutton, is the most likely candidate for the site, and therefore it could follow that it was somewhere in this area that Alfred was actually born.

The whole of Sutton seems to have been a royal vill until sometime after 1154 in the reign of Henry II. In his will, Alfred bequeathed to his successor Edward land at

167

Sutton, generally believed to be in Hampshire or in Surrey. But it could of course have been this Sutton, an important estate lying as it did close to an abbey.

It has been suggested that Hulgrove Meadow as an isolated portion of Sutton Parish indicates it to have once been a part of a much larger estate contiguous with Sutton and is consistent with fragmentation of a royal estate. But its position almost exactly halfway along the important Abingdon to Wantage highway and the gateway to the Downs suggests that it may have had a strategic importance as a half-way house.

Sutton Courtenay township controlled almost 108 acres of Hulgrove Meadow, and Sutton Wick over 58. On its western side Wantage Parish had just over 15 acres, Wantage Town had 4 acres and West Hendred Parish slightly more than 4 1/2. Why should Wantage have had land here? It has been argued that when major estates became fragmented in later Anglo-Saxon times, often at township level, it was necessary that each unit should possess the type of land necessary for a degree of self-sufficiency even if this involved the addition of detached parcels of land lying distant from the home manor. This is hardly a plausible explanantion in this case, both on account of the area's small size, its distance, and the fact that such land could have been found much closer to present Wantage along Letcombe Brook. The 15 acres belonging to Wantage Parish were almost certainly the anomalous half-virgate (approximately 15 acres) of land in the Domesday Survey under Wantage Hundred held by the King, and before 1066 by Leofled. Listed after Wantage, Charlton and Betterton; it is attributed to the Sutton revenue "but it does not belong there."

The description 'old' in the charters only refers to the final one and a half miles of Wantage Brook, the dry

168

section which still forms the parish boundary; an eastwards diversion having been made in the tenth century, or before. Signs of ancient settlement exist in the field between the old line of the brook and the diversion. 'Old' refers only to this abandoned stretch, the other charter references simply refer to 'Wantage' or 'Wantage Brook'; which would imply that there was no other Wantage for it to be confused with.

The East Hanney charters refer to it only as the "brook", except for the abandoned section which is called "old wantage" in the 968 charter. But an explanation of why the Drayton and West Hendred charters called it Wantage brook, the East Hanney charters making a single reference to Letcombe Brook as Wantage thereafter referring to the latter as "stream", could be that when the charters which have come down to us were transcribed from a twelfth century copy in the thirteenth century, or when the earlier copy was made, the scribe confronted with what we now know as Cow Common Brook as Wantage Brook thought that the wording must be an error and therefore simply called it "brook". Letcombe Brook he thought must be meant as Wantage Brook because by that time Wantage town was on Letcombe Brook. But he avoided changing the text too much by continuing to refer to it as Wantage and thereafter simply called it "stream". Thetranscribers of the Drayton and West Hendred charters had no such doubts and simply copied the original texts word for word.

"Waneting", the derivation of the name Wantage, means a "fluctuating brook", from which we obtain our modern word 'to wane'. What more logical reason therefore than to construct a dike, Mere Dike, to support a fluctuating brook (re-inforcing the lesser supply of Mydelinge brook and not Waneting brook itself). This was of course in Bronze or Iron Age times, long before the major brook had an Anglo-Saxon name.

But if there was a former Wantage here, then initially it continued to exist side by side with the new Wantage. Perhaps the first migrants left it in 871 for fear of attack by the Danes when the latter ransacked Abingdon less than four miles away. All they had to do was to go to the nearby road from Abingdon (the early Anglo-Saxon settlements were built away from the here-pæd because of the marauding war bands which used them), which led in an almost straight line to the village of Tulwick; and then continue on to Limborough, occupying the old Roman site near the more plentiful water supply offered by Letcombe Brook. A total journey of five miles. Others, we may suppose, remained, temporarily hiding in the surrounding woods and swamps.

To explain the position of the "field on the west side of Wantage" as being in the northern tip of West Hendred Parish, an alternative could be that "old Wantage" was located at the source of *Waneting broc*, east of Ardington Wick near West Hendred village. This is possible if the community wanted to keep itself separate from that of West Hendred based on Ginge Brook. But I favour as more probable the lower site, where there is evidence of extensive and long occupation and the presence of a "grove" possibly indicating a former royal residence.

Yet another alternative has been implied, that there never was another Wantage, but that the name could be applied to any stream of varying volume, such another being mentioned in Domesday Book (7). But Letcombe Brook would carry just as much water as many other brooks which did not carry the name of Waneting, although the numerous coombs and valleys on the north slopes of the Downs testify to a much higher rainfall in the past which has cut these coombs into the hillsides, and springs occasionally flow down them after wet spells representing the overflow of surplus water from the chalk. Joshua Sylvester, "The Lambourn Poet Laureate, the silver-tongued Sylvester", was well aware of these fluctuating downland streams writing in 1633:

'All Summer-long (while all thy sisters shrinke)
That of they teares a million daily drinke;
Besides thy Waste, which then in haste doth run
To wash the feet of Chaucer's Donnington:
But (while the rest are full unto the top)
All Winter-long Thou never show'st a drop,
Nor send'st a doit of need-less Subsidie,
To cramm the Kennet's Want-less Treasurie."

But we are still left with the former presence of extensive settlement of unknown name, adjacent to the real Wantage brook.

Two Wantages

If Wantage was originally sited near to Hulgrove Meadow, could this then have been the birthplace of King Alfred? It is a hundred years after Alfred's birth that we hear of two Wantage brooks, and to avoid confusion with Letcombe Brook one of these may have become known as Snodda's brook, now Cow Common Brook.

If Alfred was born at present Wantage, and if it was an important "royal residence", why did he neglect it in favour of towns such as Winchester?

Alfred married Ealhswith, daughter of Æthelred an earl of Mercia, in 868. The next year there was famine accompanied by a great mortality of both men and cattle;

171

probably from drought compounded by epidemic disease such as anthrax. This could have been the cause of the desertion of many settlements, but it seems more likely that when Abingdon was pillaged by the Danes Alfred might have fled with his young wife Ealhswith from such proximity to the enemy to a safer place, before leaving her while he went to confront the Danes at Reading. Fearing the enemy would have attacked "royal" or "old" Wantage if they were aware that any of the royal family were there.

Limborough was a more defensible position than a village in the lowland, providing a good view of any approach by the enemy along the Abingdon Road, and close also to the battle fields of the Downs. Indeed the name may derive from *lim-beorg*, Old English for "lime-tree fortress", "fortress by the wood" or "fortress by the clearing"; fortress meaning a defensible position. We saw that Alfred developed many such "burhs" or fortresses and he could have renamed it Wantage to keep alive the memory of his birthplace.

The "Royal palace" at present Wantage was simply an invention of Wise: "and here stood the Saxon palace where Alfred was born." He was probably thinking of "Asser's" remark: "What shall I say....of the royal residences, built of stone, moved from their former positions, and most beautifully set up in more fitting places by the king's command?" Archaeology has shown that there was little evidence of stone building, although seventh-century stone churches existed at Winchester and Glastonbury. The "palaces" would have been nothing more than mud and wattle with thatched roofs. But is the remark "moved from their former positions" significant? Was "Asser" thinking of another Wantage? There is no evidence of any other palace sites being moved.

We do know that Alfred initiated a strategy to extend

172

the fortresses around the borders of Wessex, with a few in the central areas. Perhaps the new Wantage was the beginnings of such a concept, later abandoned for this purpose. There is little in the archaeological record to substantiate the claim that Alfred built many palaces, and none at all to suggest that he physically moved any to new sites. But then "old Wantage" has yet to be identified and excavated.

Did Alfred have the years covering his birth expunged from the Chronicle because he wanted to obliterate all reference to "old Wantage"? The years are present regularly up to 845, then we come to this strange blank in the record. If Alfred originated the Chronicle, why was his birth not recorded in it?

We have only the single reference of "Asser" that Alfred was born at Wantage. The area was undoubtedly the king's property, and the boundary survey refers to the "king's boundary" between Grove and Hanney. In his will Alfred left present Wantage to his wife: "And to Ealhswith, the ham (= village or homestead) at Lambourn, and at Waneting, and at Ethandune." But it does not appear that his wife was living there. She died four years after Alfred and was buried at Winchester in the nunnery she had founded.

Alfred's Real Birthplace

It is my contention that a site near Hulgrove Meadow, perhaps Wantage Field itself, occupied since Bronze Age times, could have been the real site of Royal Wantage and King Alfred's birthplace, a "satellite" if you wish of Abingdon Abbey. It's name fell into desuetude after the site was abandoned because the name had followed Alfred to the new site. Alfred wanted nothing further to do with his birthplace because of his dispute with Abingdon Abbey, and may even have forbidden the use of its name. Is it not strange that not one of the Anglo-Saxon field names in the area indicates the presence of former settlement which we know existed here?

So let us summarize the argument in favour of a site in this area being the original Wantage and the birthplace of King Alfred:

1. The most telling point is that it is unlikely that ordinary migrants would have taken the name of their vill with them. That the name was transferred means that it must have had some significance since it did not describe Letcombe Brook, and the new site already had an Anglo-Saxon name, Limborough, which was changed in favour of Wantage.

2. There had been a dispute over the royal claim to Andersey Island, Anglo-Saxon kings "with devilish avarice, had unjustly built a royal building for themselves". It is conceivable that Æthelwulf placed his queen Osburh there to stake his claim to the island after the Abbey bought it back from the Mercian king in 841, and that the royal household (the queen with one or more sons, her daughter and her following of servants) were obliged to quit, leaving it in 845 in the Wessex king's absence, after the Abbey laid claim to the island following Ceolred's agreement with Beorthwulf in 844, the year before the blank in the Anglo-Saxon Chronicle begins.

3. The household could have moved straight to present Wantage, but it had no minster or abbot to provide for the queen's religious needs. If the queen had moved straight to Wantage, why take the name of Wantage to a place where it had no significance? Only later, after Alfred had become king would the name attain significance as his birthplace. It is logical to assume that the household moved to royal

lands just outside of those lands claimed by the Abbey so that the queen was not too far away from a place of worship. It was there that four years later Alfred could have been born.

Why did she not move to Drayton (if move she did), the site of another royal palace? Assuming that it was still in existence then. The answer could be that it was occupied by an underking who did not want his property taken over by the king, or that the region of Hulgrove Meadow was more important, lying as it did on the road to Limborough and close to the Marcham salt-road.

The "Sutton triangle" of Hulgrove Meadow may be significant because Sutton remained a royal vill until the reign of Henry II although the Abbey retained a holding there, so the triangle was probably royal land. It is bounded on the west by 19 acres formerly attributed to Wantage, of which about 15 belonged to the Parish and 4 to the Township. In Domesday Book 15 acres are listed as held by Leofled before 1066 in Sutton under Wantage Hundred, and noted as not belonging in the Sutton revenue. So we know that there was an early connection here with present Wantage.

4. In 871 the royal household fled to Limborough because of the proximity of the Danish threat and Alfred temporarily established his new centre there, Limborough perhaps being its first name.

5. As soon as he became king, to recover fancied loss of face, Alfred returned down the Wantage to Abingdon highway and pillaged Abingdon Abbey to avenge what he considered a wrong to his family, that of forcing it to move off land claimed as a royal residence and claimed by the Abbey under an agreement with the Mercians. At the same time he called Limborough, Wantage, to keep alive the memory of his birthplace.

So Alfred was born in the lowlands of the Vale, and it was here that he grew to manhood, hunting in the woods south of the Ock, in the flat lands between Hanney and Drayton, along the meandering old Wantage Brook and Snodda's small stream.

The legends and fantasies of the origins of Abingdon Abbey, held up for over a thousand years, have now been demolished by inquisitive historians. White Horse Hill has now been found to be a thousand years older than has been believed for the past two centuries by the most eminent scholars. And now a Professor of Mediaeval History has been bold enough to come forward and break ranks to demolish Asser's "Life of Alfred" as a thousand-year-old forgery. As to the once only "indisputable" fact concerning the legendary Alfred, Alfred, yes, I believe was born at Wantage. But at a Wantage of which the true origin is as much a mystery as is the meaning of the enigmatic White Horse.

Somewhere along old Wantage Brook, close to the Grove of the Shepherds, could lie hidden the answer to a mystery of over a thousand years waiting to be unravelled.

Notes.

1. Smyth, A.P. 1995.

2. Smyth regards this document as "suspicious".

3. Alfred's law in respect of feuds is considered to be an important step forward from barbarism, requiring that plaintiffs in a blood feud should not immediately attack or slay an accused who is in his own house but keep him

under house arrest for seven days without fighting, after which if he surrenders and gives up his weapons he is not to be harmed for another thirty days, during which his kinsmen and friends are informed giving time for reparation to be paid. Its significance here is that it establishes the existence of feuding.

4. Gibbons, A. and Davey, E.C. 1901.

5. The statue in Wantage market-place, sculpted by Count Gleichen, is said to have the face of Lord Wantage who paid for its erection. The "crown" on Alfred's head does not conform to any known Anglo-Saxon crown.

6. Wantage might have been originally included in Alfred's Burghal Hidage but no longer considered a part of the defensive strategy in the 914-919 revision. Oxford and Wallingford are included in the revised document, but not Reading. Oxford was in Mercia until 911 but annexed by Edward the Elder in that year following the death of Æthelred of Mercia.

7. Gelling, M. 1973-6.

SELECT BIBLIOGRAPHY

Anon. 1989 (1921). The Book of saints. A Dictionary of Servants of God canonized by the Catholic Church compiled by the Benedictine Monks of St. Augustine's Abbey, Ramsgate, 6th edition.

Aston, M. and Lewis, C. eds. 1994. The Mediaeval Landscape of Wessex. Oxbow Monograph 46. Oxford: Oxbow Books.

Atkinson, R.J.C. 1965. Wayland's Smithy. Antiquity. XXXIX: 126:133.

Blair, J. 1994. Anglo-Saxon Oxfordshire. Stroud: Alan Sutton.

Blair, P.H. 1960. An Introduction to Anglo-Saxon England. Cambridge: University Press.

Chesterton, G.K. 1911. The Ballad of the White Horse. London: Methuen & Co. Ltd.

Cox, M. 1986. The Story of Abingdon Part One. Privately published.

Depping, G.B., Michel, F. and Singer, S.W. 1847. Wayland Smith. A Dissertation on a Tradition of the Middle Ages. London: William Pickering.

Druce, G.C. 1897. The Flora of Berkshire. Oxford: The Clarendon Press.

Edwards, H. 1988. The Charters of the Early West Saxon
Kingdom. BAR British Series 198. Oxford: BAR.

Fitzpatrick, A.P. and Morris, E.L. eds. 1994. The Iron Age
in Wessex: Recent Work. Salisbury: Association Francaise
D'Etude de l'Age du Fer.

Gelling, M. 1973-6. The Place Names of Berkshire. 3 vols.
English Place-Name Society.

Hassall, T. 1986. The Oxford Region from the Conversion
to the Conquest. In: The Archaeology of the Oxford
Region. Eds. Briggs, G.; Cook, J. and Rowley, T. Oxford:
OU Dept. External Studies.

Hayden, E. 1908. Islands of the Vale. London: Smith, Elder
& Co.

Hooke, D. 1988. Regional Variation in Southern and
Central England in the Anglo-Saxon Period and its
Relationship to Land Units and Settlement. In: Anglo-
Saxon Settlements. Ed. Hooke, D. Oxford: Basil Blackwell.

Hughes, T. 1857. Tom Brown's Schooldays. London:
Macmillan & Co.
- 1858. The Scouring of the White Horse. London:
Macmillan & Co.1859.
- Alfred the Great. London: Macmillan & Co.

Jane, L.C. 1908. Asser's Life of King Alfred. London:
Chatto and Windus.

Keynes, S. and Lapidge, M. 1983. Alfred the Great. Asser's
Life of King Alfred and other contemporary sources.

179

London: Penguin Books.

Knott, P. 1990. Alfred's Wayte. Berkshire Old and New. (7):14-23.

Lappenburg, J.M. 1845. A History of England under the Anglo-Saxon Kings. Trans. B. Thorpe. London: John Murray.

Miles, D. and Palmer, S. 1995. White Horse Hill. Current Archaeology. XII(142):372-378.

Morgan, P. 1979. Domesday Book 5 Berkshire. Trans. A. Hawkins. Chichester: Phillimore.

Orr, J. 1918. Agriculture in Berkshire. Oxford: The Clarendon Press.

Pauli, R. 1889. The Life of Alfred the Great. Trans. B. Thorpe. London: George Bell & Sons.

Sawyer, P.H. 1968. Anglo-Saxon Charters. An Annotated List and Bibliography. London: The Royal Historical Society.

Smyth, A.P. 1995. King Alfred the Great. Oxford: Oxford University Press.

Stenton, F.M. 1913. The Early History of the Abbey of Abingdon. Oxford: B.H.Blackwell.

Stevens, J. et al. 1910. Bede's Ecclesiastical History of the English Nation. Everyman's Library. London: J.M.Dent & Sons Ltd.

Stevenson, J. 1858. Chronicon Monasterii Abingdon. 2 vols. London: Longman, Brown, Green, Longmans, and Roberts.

Stevenson, W.H. 1904. Asser's Life of King Alfred. Oxford: The Clarendon Press.

Sturdy, D. 1995. Alfred the Great. London: Constable

Whitelock, D. 1955. ed. English Historical Documents c500-1042. London: Eyre & Spottiswoode.

Wise, F. 1738. A Letter to Dr. Mead concerning some Antiquities of Berkshire. Oxford: Thomas Wood.

Woolner, D. 1967. New Light on the White Horse. Folklore. 90-111.

Also published by Llanerch:

A History of the Kings
Florence of Worcester
trans. J. Stevenson.

The Tombs of the Kings:
An Iona Book of the Dead
John Marsden.

The Chronicle of
Henry of Huntingdon
trans. T. Forester.

Roger of Wendover's
Flowers of History
trans. J. A. Giles.

Three Anglo-Saxon Battle Poems
(Finnsburh, Maldon, Brunanburh)
Trans. L. Rodrigues.

Beowulf
trans J. Porter, illus. Nick Parry.

The Kings Before the Normans
William of Malmesbury,
trans. J. Stevenson.

For a complete list of c.200 small-press editions and
facsimile reprints, write to Llanerch Publishers,
Felinfach, Lampeter, Cardiganshire, Wales, Sa48 8PJ.